JUDGING and COACHING WOMEN'S GYMNASTICS

Carolyn Osborn Bowers

National Gymnastic Judge
Member of Women's Olympic Development
Board of the United States

Jacquelyn Uphues Fie

International Gymnastic Judge
Olympian
Assistant Executive Director of the
United States Gymnastic Federation

Kitty Kjeldsen

National Gymnastic Judge
Lecturer in Physical Education,
University of Massachusetts

Andrea Bodo Schmid

International Gymnastic Judge
Olympic Gold Medalist
Associate Professor of Physical Education,
California State University, San Francisco

NATIONAL PRESS BOOKS
Palo Alto/California

Illustrations by Diana Attie Seeman

Illustration preparation supervised by Carolyn Osborn Bowers

Book design by Nancy Sears

Library of Congress Catalog Card Number: 70-142368
International Standard Book Number: 0-87484-149-6
Manufactured in the United States of America

page 11 (first line) Should read, "may not be protested *and adjusted* on this basis alone . . ."

17 (second line) Should read, "If this does occur, a 0.3 point penalty (*for each occurrence*) is taken from the team score."

71 (first line) Should read, "c. Repeating a missed element: 0.50."

72 (number 6) Penalty is: 0.1-0.2 for small error; 0.3-0.4 for medium error; 0.5 and above for serious error. Range: 0.1-1.0 point.

94 (number 1) Add: See Figure 7.1

99 Straddle Mount to Rear Support should read "Straddle Cut Mount to Rear Support"

125 (number j) Should read, "(Penalty taken from general impression or composition)"

126 (number i) Should read, "Connections (specifically turns, . . ."

134 (second line of number 7) Should read, "handstand, lower to side split or backward walkover to split between the hands. (See figure 7.18.)"

165 (figure 8.20) Legs in fourth figure must be between hand grasps in piked hang.

177 (figure 9.10) Dotted line indicates path of feet.

178 (number 1) For "(just above 40°)" read, "(just about 40°)"

180 (number 1, line 9) Should read, "The afterflight of the Yamashita must be higher than the on-flight and the distance comparable."

180 (figure 9.13) Dotted lines represent flight of body.

187 Under dimensions of equipment add, "A carpet material now covers the board for Olympic and World games, international meets, and USA national competitions. Specifications not yet available."

193 Number 16 re-evaluated after publication.

197 (under Yamashita vault) Should read,

Afterflight does not rise (hips must rise)	Up to 0.5
Insufficient opening up in afterflight	Up to 2.0
Lateness of extension in afterflight	Up to 0.5
Late execution of deep pike (back not parallel to floor)	Up to 0.5
Shortness of afterflight (looking for comparable balance)	0.3

215 (second column, first paragraph) Line 6 should read, "Points plus the 1971 Complement, and the 1972 Judging Guide for Women."

Contents

4 Mechanical Analysis of Tumbling and Apparatus Work   22

KITTY KJELDSEN

5 Dance in Gymnastics   37

CAROLYN OSBORN BOWERS

6 Floor Exercise   64

CAROLYN OSBORN BOWERS

7 Balance Beam   94

JACQUELYN UPHUES FIE

8   Uneven Parallel Bars

ANDREA BODO SCHMID

9   Vaulting

JACQUELYN UPHUES FIE AND KITTY KJELDSEN

10 Psychology of Coaching

KITTY KJELDSEN

11 Training and Certification of Judges

JACQUELYN UPHUES FIE

Illustrations

6   Floor Exercise

7   Balance Beam

8   Uneven Parallel Bars

9 Vaulting

Preface

Judging and Coaching Women's Gymnastics is the result of the authors' extensive experience in both coaching and judging in this field. The aim of the writers was to clarify the proper judging techniques and to encourage a uniformity in officiating of women's gymnastics events throughout the country.

Furthermore, it is intended to provide valuable information to coaches, teachers, and gymnasts for effective performance in their teaching and in their preparation for competition.

The authors hope that this information will assure objective and uniform assessment of routines at gymnastic competitions and will evoke ideas and practical suggestions for teaching and coaching gymnastics.

Carolyn Osborn Bowers
Jacquelyn Uphues Fie
Kitty Kjeldsen
Andrea Bodo Schmid

Introduction

ANDREA BODO SCHMID

In the past twenty years there has been an exceptional development of interest in women's competitive gymnastics in the United States: more and more junior high school, high school, and college students are participating in and observing the sport. This book has been written to interpret the FIG (*Fédération Internationale de Gymnastique*) Code of Points for Women for Olympic events and to discuss technique, composition, style, and current trends in specific areas. Coaches and gymnasts, as well as judges, should find the book invaluable in their preparation for competitions: the book will help them to understand gymnastic technique and to know what elements judges look for.

The role of judges in the practice of gymnastics is far greater than might be supposed. In their decisions and in their criticisms and explanations of the rules of competition they educate the competitors and contribute to the refinement of technique. Obviously technical understanding of each skill is of first importance to the judge, who must make decisions concerning difficulty, execution, timing, rhythm and continuity, and form. Unfortunately, training for such technical understanding has been much neglected. It is true that in recent times clinics for officials have been established to ensure objectivity in judging and standardization of rules. Nevertheless, a much greater effort must be made to train gymnastics judges and to clarify the rules of competition.

This book has been written in answer to such needs. It opens with discussion of a philosophy for judging and coaching and then attempts to interpret the FIG Code of Points for Women for each Olympic event (floor exercise, balance beam, uneven parallel bars, and vaulting) and to clarify the principles by which deviations in performance may be recognized. Specific knowledge required of the judge in each area is explained in detail. Each chapter discusses technique, composition, penalties and deductions, and new trends. The many figures illustrate perfect technique, points for evaluation, and the bases for determining the magnitude of mistakes. Each chapter includes coaching hints to increase points, and there are suggestions on coaching strategy for team competition. Chapter 11 discusses the procedure for becoming a rated gymnastic official.

Thus the book is of direct technical help to both the inexperienced and the experienced judge, and also to the coach and gymnast in preparation for competition. With it, each can understand more fully the technique of ultimate performance and can learn what is looked for in a routine and what elements affect scores.

Briefly, this work has been written to clarify the rules of competition in women's gymnastics. As such, it is hoped that the book will be of help to judges, coaches, teachers, and gymnasts in a growing field.

1

A Philosophy of Judging Gymnastics

CAROLYN OSBORN BOWERS

INTRODUCTION

Essential to the conduct of a gymnastics meet is the gymnastics judge, who has the responsibility of evaluating the performances in the events to which she has been assigned. The quality of judging at gymnastics meets has a great impact on the development of the individual gymnast, and in the future will certainly help to determine the speed with which the United States can produce teams capable of challenging for a world championship. Competent judging can encourage the interest and enthusiasm of a young gymnast, while incompetent judging may diminish her dedication to the sport.

Many coaches, gymnasts, spectators, and judges do not realize fully the influence of a judge over a period of time. Judges' decisions influence the efforts of individual gymnasts and coaches, and also the style of United States gymnastics. For this reason care must be taken to select judges who are well prepared and impartial. The subjective evaluation of performance makes constant vigilance necessary even at the international level.

Coaches and judges alike have a responsibility in setting the atmosphere of each gymnastic meet to give maximum benefit to those who are participating and to develop the ideals of the sport. A thorough understanding of rules, events, and judging techniques is necessary for all persons in the gymnastic field.

The new FIG Code of Points for Women defines each of the women's events in a uniquely feminine manner, deviating from the old attempt to mimic men's events. This new code of points should help develop a greater number of qualified judges from all countries who will improve their own national judging standards and contribute to international judging neutrality.

The entire group of gymnastics enthusiasts in the United States has a very difficult task ahead. The task involves the organization of a capable judging force. The size of the United States alone hinders communication in the application of correct and consistent judging standards. In addition, many potential judges are discouraged by the feeling that competent judging is a Herculean endeavor. These people must be introduced to judging in a manner which will increase their understanding and confidence. A judge's ability is brought to fruition by preparedness, practice, and cooperation within the meet situation. The beginning judge must be allowed to recognize her mistakes without the pressure of hostility. She should gain her experience at beginning meets where the pressure for complete success in performance should not be upon the gymnast either.

RELATIONSHIP OF JUDGING TO COMPETITORS

This section deals with the relationship between judges and individual competitors and coaches. It discusses the relationship of judging to the selection of United

States teams and it delineates a judge's specific responsibilities. It is hoped that the discussion will help to produce a truly competitive atmosphere, which is more helpful to all involved than one in which hostility is directed to those giving of their time and effort in judging.

Accurate judging definitely aids the development of quality performances. Competitive scores can be a tremendous incentive to the competitor, but only when her progress is accurately recorded. If local judges score a beginner higher than the correct value for the routine performed, there will inevitably be a day of reckoning when further effort and progress are discouraged. The performer who receives erroneously high scores because she is the best in a meet will nevertheless reach a higher level of competition when her routines are *correctly* evaluated. Many potential gymnasts have been unable to accept the large drop in scores resulting from such misdirected benevolence. The failure to understand this often precipitates the resignation of potential gymnasts from competition.

Judging may also influence the training of a gymnast. On the basis of a judge's evaluation, a coach may or may not make wise decisions regarding a competitor's performance. The coach should have the benefit of accurate scores to facilitate the development of a gymnast. Both the coach and judge must have a thorough understanding of FIG standards for the total performance.

There are only a few coaches in the United States today who can make informed and objective application of the rules to the performance of a gymnast. This is partly due to the wide disparity in judging interpretation and standards. It may also be because the coach does not function sufficiently within the judging atmosphere. Many coaches are overly influenced by close association with gymnasts and also fail to understand the importance of the total composition of an event. For example, some scores elicit furious arguments from coaches who disagree solely

on the basis of difficulties performed. These coaches ignore entirely the other six points for evaluation. It is possible to score less than four points, for example, even when all difficulties are performed, if proper deductions are made for falls, spotting, and failure to execute the difficulty completely. The coach must not be blinded by the execution of a group of stunts or by one facet of a routine.

Local and regional judges can have positive influence on coaches and gymnasts only when they strive to maintain the standards of national judges. Therefore, they must follow FIG standards in order to insure equivalent scores for identical performances in any region of the United States. The coaches have a right to demand this, but they must also help to nurture accurate judging by greater understanding and fewer verbal assaults. The coach must place values in perspective. Moving up one place in one small meet by argument may not be nearly as valuable as trying to understand the causes of a judge's reaction. By working with the judges, a coach can determine a judge's reaction to the style and composition of a routine. When coaches disagree with local judges, they should try to arrange for national help on a workshop basis involving both coaches and judges. Only cooperation will promote knowledge and growth.

Judges often disagree on the question of providing critical analysis to a competitor or coach. A reluctance against discussion has prevailed in the past because of the tone of most inquiry. The individual judge, however, can be a valuable resource to the gymnast when the meet situation allows time and the inquiry is sincere. Depending upon the type of question asked, a judge may either answer a question directly or refer the coach to a superior judge.

Each judge must always be able to justify her score to her superior judge. She can use this training for contribution to the development of performers. The judge can train herself, for example, to remember each performance from her tally sheet comments. A quick explanation of the breakdown of the FIG formula may help a gymnast in the future. The need for cooperation between judges, coaches, and competitors is very great at present because of the rapid growth of the sport's popularity and the consequent shortage of coaches.

RELATIONSHIP OF JUDGES TO UNITED STATES TEAMS

The gymnastic judge at any level must be deeply involved with the sport. She must study compulsory exercises and maintain familiarity with the latest trends in gymnastics prior to every judging commitment. By virtue of the scores they give in local and regional meets, judges can help coaches and gymnasts to realize when they are ready to enter national competition. Scores which are a truthful measure of ability separate those who should move up to a higher level of competition from those who ought to compete only at lower levels. When all judging becomes consistent, it stands to reason that the gymnasts who are truly best will reach the national senior competitions. Selection of national teams will be facilitated when the judges at senior national competitions are not overburdened with poorly performed routines.

RESPONSIBILITIES OF A JUDGE

A judge should arrive at the meet site in time to confer with the other judges, the superior judge, and the meet director. She should prepare for judging compulsory exercises by walking through and mentally reviewing each exercise many times prior to the meet date. She should be able to recognize each exercise in reverse performance as well as from the designated text. Floor patterns and directions must be recognized from any of the possible starting places.

A judge must be informed about any rule changes. The judges should discuss rule changes with the meet director in order to be prepared for the meet situation.

For example, if the value of a vault has been changed, the information should normally be given to the competitors a few weeks prior to the meet. If, however, the change has been recent and not well publicized, the meet may possibly be run utilizing the former vault value. These decisions should be announced by the meet director and the judges should act accordingly.

A judge should present herself in a professional manner. Her position is such that she should have a neat and pleasant appearance. She should not attempt to be the center of attention by extreme dress, hair style, or actions. She should dress in a uniform when requested. A standard uniform may be a dark skirt and white blouse.

A judge should have the self-assurance resulting from the fact that she has prepared for each meet. She must be ready to judge both compulsory and optional routines in the events to which she has been assigned. The judge should feel qualified to give the competitors consistent performance appraisals.

A judge, of course, should be free from bias and should try to perform her duties to the best of her ability at each meet. She should face the challenge of her responsibilities as a judge by developing:

1. The ability to recognize the correct execution of all skills and the effects of mistakes on the total performance.
    a. The ability to recognize the utmost possible amplitude of each separate movement.
    b. The ability to evaluate physical differences (for example, differences in height as they affect the evaluation of amplitude for leaps and jumps).
2. The ability to remember all of the rules and regulations, to interpret these rules and regulations during an actual performance, and to make rapid decisions following a performance.
3. The ability to recognize medium and superior difficulties and to recognize when technical performance should lower the difficulty value.

4. The ability to remain unbiased.
5. The ability to remain consistent in judgment during long sessions.
6. The ability to recognize the value of a total composition, within the set limits of the rules; for this a judge must develop sensitivity to many qualities of movement, appreciation of artistic design, and recognition of excellence in the execution of transitions.
7. The ability to interpret written compulsory routines fully and accurately and a willingness to learn these routines thoroughly.

It is difficult for a beginning judge who feels uncomfortable in the judging position to accept the responsibility of actually judging a meet. It is true that training at institutes and workshops and the use of rating tests are aids to the development of a judge. Nevertheless, there is still no substitute for judging experience. Consistency during an event is the first step toward confidence. A mistake made because of lack of understanding will at least affect each competitor equally. This small comfort, however, should not impede the judge's readiness to study and improve. The very best judges are not always completely comfortable, simply because of the nature of passing judgment on others. The satisfaction should be that each honest effort provides service to the growing sport of gymnastics.

2
A Philosophy of Coaching Gymnastics

KITTY KJELDSEN

Much has been written in recent years about the philosophy of education. New and unorthodox points of view are emerging from many directions. The prevailing trend is in the direction of individualized education, with an almost tailor-made curriculum for each student, based on need and interest. The implementation of this philosophy requires smaller student-teacher ratios, more up-to-date equipment, and more thorough teacher preparation.

There are definite similarities between this and the modern philosophy of coaching individual sports: particularly gymnastics. This philosophy encourages, for example, specialization, the pursuit of excellence, individualized student-teacher contacts, and in-depth teacher preparation. It requires a small student-teacher ratio and a certain amount of specialized equipment. Like the new trends in education, it does not come cheaply or allow much provision for large groups. Like the new trends in education, it can create tremendous excitement and dedication among a small number of people, and can give them the most rewarding of experiences. It certainly is not a philosophy that stresses routine procedures for the sake of efficiency. Such coaching is very much needed for the small group of really talented people in our school population. This group has for a long time been the stepchild of our physical education program. We have been using these girls as "student leaders," which is just another name for "assistant teachers," in order to make our job of handling large classes easier. We have customarily encouraged them to learn other new sports,

instead of giving them in-depth training in their specialty. Above all, until recently we have succeeded in making them feel guilty over specialization and have driven many of them into outside clubs and teams for the inspiration and experience that should have been provided within the school system.

In order to implement this new coaching philosophy, many of us must rid ourselves of habits acquired in our own teacher-training days. We must stop feeling guilty for spending our time with a relatively small number of girls, and above all, we should stop forcing everybody into the mold of "jack-of-all-trades and master-of-none." There is nothing wrong with being a jack-of-all-trades. On the other hand, there is nothing wrong with specialization, as long as the student and teacher both realize the sacrifices that must be made.

Just as every student is not interested or successful in specializing in one activity to the exclusion of several others, not every teacher will make a successful coach. Becoming a coach should be, as much as possible, a free choice of the teacher and not another assigned activity such as an extra lunch duty or class. Very often academic teachers who were skilled team members in their undergraduate years will make better coaches than unmotivated physical educators. This resource should be tapped more often in the future, especially since a greater number of high schools and colleges are starting teams in women's individual sports.

As mentioned at the beginning, the philosophy of

coaching involves dedication and the pursuit of excellence. Without the first, the second cannot be achieved. The student should be dedicated to the point of excluding many other things she would like to do with her free time. That time must be spent in the gymnasium, perfecting physical skills in the sport of her choice. She should be taught to work beyond her first perception of fatigue, since only by putting an overload on her muscles will she improve their condition. She should be willing to follow the prescribed diet, training schedule, or other daily routine best in her particular situation, and she must guard against discouragement when she is faced with difficulties. At this point real dedication is tested. On the other hand, we usually find that no matter how great her initial enthusiasm, a student's efforts are short-lived unless her teacher or coach is willing to match her dedication, feat by feat. A coach who is not willing to give all of herself cannot expect full dedication from her students. Neither can she succeed if her dedication is only superficial; the student will sense it very soon.

Sometimes, despite her dedication, the situation in which the teacher finds herself is not conducive to successful coaching. For example, she may be so overloaded with classwork and expected to take care of so many other extra things that by the time she gets to the gymnastics practice she has nothing left to give. On the other hand, a coach's personal interests may be so important to her that she cannot wait for the appointed team practice to be over and leaves the gymnasium as early as possible. More often than not, the best learning situations do not go by the clock. True coaching can never be a nine-to-five activity. It is a way of life for the student *and* the teacher. Teachers who are not willing to give it their full dedication will never succeed in bringing the highest possible potential out of their students. They will just be playing at coaching and so producing situations that are emotionally satisfying to neither party.

Often the worst deterrent to good coaching is the unbending attitude which many administrators and physical educators themselves have toward specialization and the pursuit of excellence in girls' activities. They claim that such specialization gives young women an unsound philosophy on life. Coaches are often made to believe that in paying special attention to an exceptionally talented small group of people, they are neglecting the others and keeping them from rich and rewarding physical experiences. Nevertheless, the trend in the entire educational system is toward small groups, individualized attention, and in-depth studies in specialized fields. In the classroom we are paying more and more attention to the gifted student, providing him or her with special accelerated classes and other opportunities for advanced study; the precedent has already been set to develop the gifted to the extent of their capacity. Is a coach in physical education really doing something so different? Why should she feel guilty in doing what enlightened academic teachers have been striving for in recent years?

A philosophy of coaching cannot exist in a vacuum. In order to be workable, it must agree at least partly with the philosophy of education of the coach's particular school. There must be give and take between administrators and coaches. The coach, for example, should recognize the importance of a solid general physical education program for all members of the institution. This is the background, after all, for individualized instruction.

The administrators, on the other hand, should recognize the need for in-depth specialization and make room for it in the total program. Every effort should be made to make clear to the administrator that some activities by nature need more time for the pursuit of excellence than others. The total conditioning and overall effort needed for success in gymnastics keeps it from becoming a short seasonal sport. Working all year with a gymnastic group is not necessarily an example of overemphasis; often it is the *only* way of achieving a fully satisfying experience—the only way of helping talented girls to achieve their potential. If the school situation makes gymnastics a seasonal sport, lesser results must be expected by everyone involved— a situation less than satisfying to the really dedicated student and coach. In this case, the importance of outside gymnastics groups and programs connected with recreational institutions should not be overlooked. They could be the answer for a really serious girl, and she should be able to supplement her training there without violating school regulations.

Administrators should also realize that a physical educator cannot successfully coach more than one sport during a season and that the coaching of gymnastics requires a specialized background not obtainable as readily as skills in coaching today's most popular team sports. To increase her knowledge, the gymnastic coach should be encouraged to attend clinics, with free time and financial support given by the school that has hired her and plans to utilize her talents during the season ahead.

Above all, women physical educators should realize the value of specialized coaching within a program of general physical education. The specialized coaching effort is not necessarily an example of overemphasis; it is the attempt to develop a talent fully. A sound coaching philosophy and pursuit of excellence are characteristic of the times, and should be recognized as important tools for the development of today's younger generation.

3

The FIG Code*

JACQUELYN UPHUES FIE

The FIG Code of Points was developed for the exact purpose of evaluating exercises during competitions conducted on the international, continental, and national levels. We are faced with the difficult task of evaluating gymnastic performance on all ability levels using this same set of rules and regulations.

In Europe there seems to be no difficulty encountered in the application of the FIG Code. The competitive system is so structured that gymnasts performing optional routines are definitely "ready." These girls have advanced through a system of compulsory gymnastic competitions to a level that exhibits preparedness, security, and mastery of performance at intermediate through advanced levels. It is indeed a rare instance to witness a score below 6.0 points during competition.

The many judging difficulties, questions, and uneasy situations that arise in the United States are caused often by the inadequate preparation of judges but even more by the inadequate preparation of the many gymnasts. Our national system is now so structured that these extremely difficult judging situations will soon be eliminated. We look forward to the day when only those girls that can do justice to a compulsory and/or optional routine are encouraged or allowed to enter competition.

Gymnastic performance is now evaluated by four judges who compute their scores without consultation or comparison. One brief consultation period after the first exercise is allowed during the preliminary competition. At this time the judges exchange views regarding deductions for all aspects of the exercise performed. They attempt to set the standards to which they must strictly adhere throughout the entire judging period at that event. The judge must mentally refer to this first score periodically or when necessary in order to remain consistent. However, one should not judge each successive performance by comparing deductions with the previous routine, as overall perspective and consistency is then lost.

If a judge becomes inconsistent, she alters the correct placing of all gymnasts in that particular event and the overall scores in the all-around event. If such repeated inconsistency occurs, the judge may be removed by action of the superior judge and the jury.

Additional judges are required to serve as line judges for the floor exercise, time judges for the floor exercise and beam, and judges concerned with the exact number and chronological order of the elements in the compulsory exercises. These judges signal to the head judge after the exercise is completed if a violation has occurred.

A fifth judge also observes team performance during the optional exercises. This control judge checks mounts, dismounts, similarity of exercises, and types of vaults among team members.

*The official *FIG Code of Points for Women* is available through the United States Gymnastic Federation, Box 4699, Tucson, Arizona 85717. The price is $5.50 (including the *FIG Supplement*).

The superior judge must check all four scores and be sure that the two middle scores fall within the proper range for preliminary competition, as follows: •

> 0.30 point for scores from 9.50 to 10.00 points
> 0.50 point for scores from 8.50 to 9.45 points
> 1.00 point for all other score ranges

For final competition this range for scores is:

> 0.20 point for scores from 9.50 to 10.00 points
> 0.30 point for scores from 8.50 to 9.45 points
> 0.50 point for scores from 7.00 to 8.45 points
> 1.00 point for all score ranges

After the two middle scores are averaged, the superior judge takes any additional deductions for time-limit or line violations from this average score. The resultant score is flashed to the gymnasts, coaches, and general audience.

If the two middle scores are out of line with the FIG point spread for preliminary or final competition, the superior judge calls a conference, reviews the routine, and gives her score. The middle score furthest from the score of the superior judge must be adjusted so that the scores fall within the range.

Examples of Preliminary point difference:

1. Superior score: 7.4 (1.0 range)
   Middle scores: 6.5 and 7.6
   The 6.5 score must adjust to at least 6.6 to bring the scores in line.
   Average: 6.6 and 7.6 = 7.1

2. Superior score: 8.9 (0.5 range)
   Middle scores: 9.0 and 8.4
   The 8.4 score must adjust to at least 8.5 to bring the scores in line.
   Average: 9.0 and 8.5 = 8.75

The average score must also be in line with the score of the superior judge according to the FIG point differences:

	Superior Judge's Score	Average Score
Prelims	9.5 to 10.00	within 0.3
	8.5 to 9.45	within 0.5
	Below 8.50	within 1.0
Finals	9.5 to 10.00	within 0.2
	8.5 to 9.45	within 0.3
	7.0 to 8.45	within 0.5
	Below 7.00	within 1.0

The FIG approved method for score adjustment in the U.S.A. is as follows:

If the average score is out of line with the score of the superior judge, the gymnast's score is computed *without* consultation in the following manner:

1. The two middle scores are averaged.
2. This average score is added to the score of the superior judge.
3. This total is divided by two to arrive at the final base score for the gymnast. This score is flashed.

Example of Final point differences:

	Superior Score	Average Score	Base Score
Case No. 1	9.8 (0.2 range)	9.5	$19.3/2 = 9.65$
Case No. 2	9.0 (0.3 range)	8.6	$17.6/2 = 8.80$
Case No. 3	9.1 (0.3 range)	9.5	$18.6/2 = 9.30$

In case of *protest*, after review and decision by the jury, the meet referee or president of the jury *may* alter the score by one of two methods. When using the first method:

1. Take the score of the four individual scores that is the highest.
2. Add this score to that of the superior judge.
3. Average the total to arrive at the adjusted score.

Example:	Individual Scores	Superior Score	Adjusted Score
Case No. 1	9.0, 9.1, 9.3, 9.3	9.3	$18.6/2 = 9.30$
Case No. 2	9.0, 9.1, 9.3, 9.3	9.0	$18.3/2 = 9.15$

The second method uses the base score method of averaging the score of the superior judge and the average score. In case No. 2, the adjusted score works out to be less than the average score. The coach is bound by the final decision of the jury. In a rare instance, after jury deliberation, the meet referee may counsel the superior judge if her score seems inaccurate. Internationally, if the judge (or judges) refuses to change her score when out of line, the superior judge may flash her score as the average score.

A coach may protest the score of her own gymnast only in comparison to the first score of the competition, which serves as the evaluation of the technical level of the competition. The coach may not protest in comparison to another gymnast's score specifically. She may state reasons why she feels that her own gymnast's score should be higher, specifying areas of originality, composition, difficulty, general impression, amplitude, and execution as compared to the general level of all categories in the meet. Serious problems would occur if protests were made with reference to any other gymnast's score. For example, if gymnast number 23 was over-scored, subsequent scores may not be protested on this basis alone or the entire meet scoring and all-around scores would be thrown off. An occasional under- or over-score does occur, for reasons too many to list. However, further scores must not be based on the mistake or the error would be magnified. All judging is based on the first score, which provides the common ground or basis for subsequent scoring in the event.

Prior to each U.S.A. gymnastic meet of any size, an appropriate jury must be selected. It is recommended that the jury consist of the following representatives:

1. Superior judge of the event in question.
2. Meet director.
3. Two predesignated judges possessing the highest rating of the group.
4. President of jury (president of technical committee), meet referee, or head of all judges for the entire competition.

The rules for selection of the jury during national meets have been developed by the various national organizations: the AAU, DGWS, and USGF.

Individual scores are not flashed anymore. Only the average of the two middle scores is made known to gymnast and the public. This, it is hoped, will prevent antagonistic feelings between coaches, gymnasts, and judges. Judges themselves cannot be influenced by each other's individual scores.

NATIONAL JUDGING OF COMPULSORY EXERCISES

With the exception of the horse vault, each compulsory exercise may be performed only once. To evaluate the compulsory exercise from zero to 10 points the following formula is used:

4 points for content, subdivided as follows:

Exactness and correctness of all parts of exercise	2.0
Exactness and precision of direction of floor pattern	0.5
Exactness of rhythm of exercise	1.5

6 points for execution, subdivided as follows:

Elegance of execution	1.0
Coordination of movements and body parts	1.0
Lightness of leaps, jumps, and acrobatics	1.0
Amplitude of movement	1.5
Sureness of execution	1.5

For sample judge's worksheets, see figures 3.1 and 3.2.

EVENT_____   NAME OF JUDGE_____

COMPETITOR_____

Scratch Area	Value	Breakdown	Deductions
	2.0	Exactness of Parts	
	0.5	Precision of Direction and Floor Pattern	
	1.5	Exactness of Rhythm	
	1.0	Elegance	
	1.0	Coordination	
	1.0	Lightness	
	1.5	Amplitude	
	1.5	Sureness	
		Falls	
		Neutral Deductions	
		TOTAL DEDUCTIONS	
		FINAL SCORE	

3.1   Sample Judge's Worksheet, Compulsory Exercise

EVENT_____   NAME OF JUDGE_____

COMPETITOR_____

Scratch Area		
	Exactness of Text (2.0)	
	Direction and Floor Pattern (0.5)	
	Rhythm (1.5)	
	Elegance (1.0)	
	Coordination (1.0)	
	Lightness (1.0)	
	Amplitude (1.5)	
	Sureness (1.5)	
	SCORE	
	Falls, Neutral Deductions	
	FINAL SCORE	

3.2   Sample Judge's Worksheet, Compulsory Exercise

The following more detailed examination of this breakdown will clarify the categories of deductions and penalties:

Exactness and Correctness of All Parts of Exercise

The total of 2.0 points is broken down as follows:

Omitting a medium element 0.5
Omitting a superior element 1.0
Changing a small or easy part 0.1
Reversing an acrobatic or tumbling element 0.5
Reversing an easy part 0.2

If in the National Compulsory Routines for Girls there are no superior elements in any event, a one-point deduction for omitting a superior element cannot occur. Those elements constituting difficulty in the medium class are penalized by 0.5 point if omitted. For those movements constituting a major part of the compulsory exercise but not classified as medium difficulties (such as a handstand-forward roll in a beginning level floor exercise), appropriate deductions in accordance with the table of penalties for that exercise must be made.

Exactness and Precision of Direction of Floor Pattern

The total of 0.5 point is broken down as follows:

Minor directional errors .... 0.1 to 0.2
Major directional errors .... 0.3 to 0.5

It must be kept in mind that the total deduction is only 0.5 point. To lose 0.3 point for directional errors would indicate that approximately half of the routine was done in the wrong direction.

Exactness of Rhythm of Exercise

The total of 1.5 points is broken down as follows:

Music too slow .... Up to 0.5
Pianist must wait for gymnast .... Up to 0.5
Pianist aids gymnast .... Up to 0.5
Music in wrong rhythm .... Up to 1.5
Slight stops in rhythm (per stop) 0.2
Decided lack of rhythm per section 0.3
Overall rhythm abrupt and jerky 0.5

The last three penalties refer to floor exrcise, beam, and uneven bars.

Elegance of Execution

An elegant performance exhibits grace, poise, expressivity, presence, and maturity of movement. A total of 1.0 point is given. Deductions range from 0.1-0.2 for a small error, 0.3-0.4 for a medium error, and 0.5 and above for a serious error.

Coordination of Movements and Body Parts

A coordinated performance is characterized by fluent, rhythmical, and smooth movement of the body, head, arms, and legs.

The total of 1.0 point is broken down as follows:

Small lack .... 0.1 to 0.2

Medium lack .... 0.3 to 0.4

Serious lack .... 0.5 and above

Lightness of Leaps, Jumps, and Acrobatics

A total of 1.0 point is given. Specific deductions are as follows:

Landing without suppleness and with noise 0.1

Heavy landing 0.2

Amplitude of Movements

The term "amplitude" refers to the largeness and fullness of the gymnast's performance. The total of 1.5 points is broken down as follows:

Each fault (in medium and superior difficulties only) 0.2

Slight lack of amplitude in general 0.2

Pronounced lack (in general) 0.3

Total lack (in general) 1.5

The overall evaluation of amplitude is made at the end of the performance.

Sureness of Execution

This term refers to specific faults, breaks, and errors in execution as defined in Article XI in the FIG Code of Points and the Table of Penalties for Compulsory Exercises.

For general faults, total of 1.5 points is broken down as follows:

Small faults .... 0.1 to 0.2

Medium faults .... 0.3 to 0.4

Serious faults .... 0.5 and above

Evaluation of the compulsory horse vault is treated in the chapter on vaulting.

INTERNATIONAL JUDGING OF COMPULSORY EXERCISES

Beginning with the Olympic Games in 1972, each nation will perform a different compulsory composition incorporating the prescribed compulsory elements. In order to evaluate the originality of the combinations, the pattern of the movement, the musical accompaniment, and the harmony and rhythm of the music and the movement, a change in the point breakdown of the area of composition has been made.

These points are divided as follows:

Precision of all compulsory elements 2.0

Variety and richness of connections 1.5

General rhythm of exercise 0.5

Penalties to be applied with this new system are:

Omission of one medium difficulty 0.5

Omission of one superior difficulty 1.0

Changing order of elements, per element 0.3

Acrobatic elements executed in addition to compulsory elements,

per element 0.5

The regulations, penalties, and point breakdown for the compulsory horse vault have remained the same.

The duration of the exercises on the floor and on the beam will be prescribed by the FIG Technical Committee. The timing procedures, regulations, and resulting penalties will remain the same as those for the optional exercises.

During the performances on the floor, beam and uneven bars a fifth judge takes her place near the head or superior judge. She communicates to the head judge if there is a deviation from the prescribed number or chronological order or the elements. The appropriate penalty is taken from the average score by the head judge.

JUDGING OF OPTIONAL EXERCISES

As in the compulsory exercises, each optional exercise on the bars, the beam, and the floor may be performed only once. To evaluate the optional exercise from zero to 10 points the following formula is used:

6 points for composition, subdivided as follows:

Difficulty (two movements of superior difficulty worth 1.0 point each, and four movements of medium difficulty worth 0.5 point each) 4.0

Originality and value of combinations and connections 1.5

General impression of the composition and structure of exercise 0.5

4 points for execution, subdivided as follows:

Technical execution 1.5

Amplitude of movement.. 1.5

General impression 1.0

For sample judge's worksheets, see figures 3.3 and 3.4.

The fifth judge or control judge checks that not more than two members of the same team execute the same mount and/or dismount. If such an infraction occurs, a 0.3 point penalty is taken from the team total. The control judge also checks that

EVENT_____   NAME OF JUDGE_____

COMPETITOR_____

Scratch Area	Value	Breakdown	Deductions
	4.0	Difficulty	
	1.5	Originality—Combinations	
	0.5	Composition	
	1.5	Technical Execution	
	1.5	Amplitude	
	1.0	General Impression	
		Neutral Deductions	
		Falls	
		TOTAL DEDUCTIONS	
		FINAL SCORE	

3.3   Sample Judge's Worksheet, Optional Exercise

EVENT_____   NAME OF JUDGE_____

COMPETITOR_____

Scratch Area		
	Difficulty (4.0)	
	Originality (1.5)	
	Composition (0.5)	
	Execution (1.5)	
	Amplitude (1.5)	
	General Impression (1.0)	
	SCORE	
	Falls, Neutral Deductions	
	FINAL SCORE	

3.4   Sample Judge's Worksheet, Optional Exercise

from the twelve vaults performed by each team not more than four vaults are the same. If this does occurs, a 0.3 point penalty is taken from the team score.

The following more detailed examination of this breakdown will clarify the categories of deductions and penalties:

Difficulty

It is highly recommended that difficulties beyond the required number be added *cautiously,* as this exposes the gymnast to more faults and deductions. Gymnasts of lower caliber should do what they are capable of with perfection. They should not attempt what is not perfected or cannot be performed with absolute sureness. Full or partial credit for difficulty is earned by executing these combinations of superior and medium difficulties:

2 superiors 2.0	4.0	(Deductions under composition applicable to beam and floor only.)
4 mediums 2.0		
4 superiors 4.0	4.0	(with a deduction under composition of 0.5 for an unbalanced exercise according to the regulations.)
0 mediums 0.0		
1 superior 1.0	3.0	(with a deduction under composition of 0.2 for the exercise not conforming to the regulations.)
6 mediums 2.0		
0 superiors 0.0	2.0	(with a deduction under composition of 0.5 for the composition not conforming to the regulations.)
8 mediums 2.0		

To generalize the above regulations:

1. It is possible to earn only 2.0 points for any number of medium difficult moves.
2. At no time may a superior difficulty be replaced by additional medium difficulties.
3. It is possible to earn 1.0 points for each superior move, the total of which may not exceed four points for the total difficulty credit.
4. Specific to the balance beam and the floor exercise:
   a. If the exercise contains one, two, or three elements of medium difficulty, a penalty of 0.2 point is taken from the composition for the exercise not conforming to the logical balance.

b. If the exercise contains only one element of superior difficulty, a 0.2 penalty is taken.

c. If the exercise contains no medium elements or no superior elements, a 0.5 penalty is taken from the composition.

5. A penalty under composition may be assessed on the uneven bars, if the judge feels that the exercise is unbalanced as a result of too many continuous superior movements.

Penalties regarding difficulties are as follows:

Difficulty repeated more than three times in succession 0.1
(with the exception of the backhand spring)

Fall during execution of difficulty (incomplete) .... No credit

Fall when difficulty is almost complete .... Difficulty given credit, but deductions are taken for fall or serious error

Originality and Value of Combinations and Connections and General Impression of Composition and Structure of Exercise

The gymnast must execute all the recommended techniques and elements, showing a balanced routine. Penalties not exceeding 2.0 points may be assessed as follows:

Lack of (or excess of) one type of movement
(each infraction) .... 0.1 to 0.2
Examples:

1. A beam exercise showing too many variations of the inverted support-handstand.

2. A bar exercise containing an excess number of glide kips or reverse kipping movements.

3. A floor exercise in which turns or pivots are performed in the same direction and style throughout.

Exercises showing only one type of movement (example: flexibilities) .... Up to 0.5

Masculine movements or appearance of exercise (Do not penalize again under General Impression.) .... Up to 1.5

Originality and difficulty of combinations not up to level of difficulty of competition .... Up to 0.5

Lack of originality in otherwise good routine 0.2

Poor connections 0.3

Lack of originality in poor routine 0.5

Lack of originality whatsoever 1.5

Repetition of a compulsory element with the same links before and after 0.3

Combinations too difficult or unsuitable for gymnast .... Up to 0.5
Mount not up to difficulty of routine in general .... Up to 0.2
Dismount not up to difficulty of routine in general .... Up to 0.3
Difficulties not placed progressively throughout routine .... Up to 0.5
All difficulty in first part of exercise .... Up to 0.3
Failure to use entire area (floor, beam, or bars) .... Up to 0.5

Technical Execution

The total number of points is 1.5. General faults in execution are listed in the summary of general faults below. Specific penalties are covered in the chapters dealing with specific apparatus.

Amplitude of Movement

The total of 1.5 points is subdivided as follows:

Each fault (difficulties) 0.2
Slight overall lack of amplitude 0.2
Pronounced lack during major section for sequence 0.3
Total lack 1.5

General Impression

Gymnasts draw deductions in this category for:

Lack of lightness and easy execution.

Lack of expressive and dynamic performance.

Lack of beauty, grace, and elegance in movement.

Lack of ability to perform fluently and rhythmically with coordination in accordance with body structure.

Undesirable appearance, presentation, and posture.

Deductions are made in line with the severity of deductions in other categories.

The total of 1.0 is subdivided as follows:

Small fault .... 0.1 to 0.2
Medium fault .... 0.3 to 0.4
Serious fault .... 0.5 and above

SUMMARY OF GENERAL DEDUCTIONS
Deductions for General Faults in Execution and Amplitude
for All Movements and Landings

Small faults .... 0.1 to 0.2

1. Head or toes incorrectly positioned.
2. Small bend in the arms, legs, or body (trunk).
3. Slight straddling of the legs (up to 45°).
4. Landings without suppleness.

5. Touching floor lightly with one or two feet.
6. Slight loss of balance on landings.
7. Slight alternate hand supports when undesirable.
8. Slight stops in rhythm.
9. Slight lack of amplitude.

Medium faults .... 0.3 to 0.4
1. Definite bending of arms, legs, or body.
2. Straddling of legs (45°-90°).
3. Undesirable movements of the arms or trunk in order to stay in balance.
4. Definite and obvious lack of continuity between movements.
5. Supplementary leg support on side of beam.
6. Alternate hand placement when undesirable.
7. Definite lack of amplitude.

Serious faults .... 0.5 and above
1. Severe bending of the arms, legs, or body.
2. Severe straddling of the legs (over 90°).
3. Supplementary support of fingers, hands, or body on floor or apparatus.
4. Overall jerky execution.
5. Serious lack of amplitude throughout the exercise.

Deductions for Falls and Assists Between Spotter and Gymnast

	Bar Penalty	Beam Penalty
Fall from apparatus	1.0	0.5
During fall on dismount, coach assists or catches gymnast	1.5	1.5
Coach assists gymnast on dismount after the difficulty is completed or as she arrives on ground	0.5	0.5
Intentional touch by coach, even if slight, with little or no aid resulting	1.5	1.5
Unintentional touch by coach	No penalty unless touch causes another execution fault	
Intentional touch by gymnast on coach for aid, even if slight	1.5	1.5
Unintentional touch by gymnast on coach	No penalty unless touch causes another execution penalty	

Neutral Deductions

Frequently penalties do not fall specifically into any of the three common execution categories: technical execution, amplitude, or general impression. In the U.S.A. such penalties are often called "neutral deductions" and are subtracted from the final score by the individual judge before it is conveyed to the superior judge. Neutral deductions pertain to the following:

> Speech, action, or placement of the coach and/or performer, including all penalties for assists and touches.
>
> Fall on apparatus or to the floor.
>
> Initial contact with apparatus without mounting or beginning routine.

Penalties related to the following items are subtracted from the average score by the superior judge:

> Gymnast warming up on apparatus during consultation of judges.
>
> Attire of the gymnast.
>
> Area restrictions in floor exercise.
>
> Time restrictions in balance beam and floor exercise.

The faults listed above, together with all additional faults, are described more fully in the following chapters.

4

Mechanical Analysis of Tumbling and Apparatus Work

KITTY KJELDSEN

An understanding of the mechanics involved can be very helpful in the practice of tumbling and apparatus work. Regardless of individual bodily differences, the principles of mechanics apply to all bodies in movement. Knowledge of these principles will greatly help in analyzing the skills to be mastered in tumbling, vaulting, floor exercise, or work with other apparatus. Understanding of such principles is of equal value to the gymnast, coach, and judge; moves can be executed less effortfully, mistakes can be corrected more readily, and good techniques can be distinguished from poorer but perhaps flashier ones.

This chapter begins with a short glossary of terms and proceeds with sections discussing individual principles. Each section begins with a statement of the principle and continues with an interpretation and examples. The chapter concludes with an analysis of selected tumbling and acrobatic stunts.

GLOSSARY OF TERMS

Acceleration: an increase in speed or velocity.

Angular momentum: the force or speed of angular movement.

Angular velocity: the time rate of change of angular motion.

Axis: a line about which a rotating body turns.

Center of gravity: the imaginary point in a body at which its whole weight is concentrated.

Momentum: force or speed of movement.

Pendulum: a body so suspended from a fixed point as to move to and fro by the action of gravity and acquired momentum.

Radius of rotation: the distance between the center of gravity of a rotating body and the point around which it rotates.

Rotation: angular motion in which all parts of the body move in a circular path about an axis.

Velocity: rapidity of motion.

MECHANICAL PRINCIPLES
Conditions of Balance

The principles to be discussed are these:

1. The lower the location of the center of gravity, the more stable the body.
2. The wider the base of support, the more stable the body.

The center of gravity of a body is the point at which its whole weight can be imagined as being concentrated. In the human body standing in an upright position, the center of gravity is generally in the hip region and varies slightly with individual body build. Any change in the shape or position of the body or in the distribution of its mass will change the location of the center of gravity. The center of gravity can be inside or outside of the body, but as long as it remains over the base of support, the body is in balance.

The more stable the body, the stronger the force required to move it. Therefore, light tumbling requires a

4.1 Approximate Locations of Center of Gravity in Different Body Positions

slightly unstable position. This slightly off-balance position is especially important in some take-off positions, such as sitting back in preparation for a back handspring. Tumbling with the body in either a stable position or one too unstable will result in slow, laborious work or low, stumbling movements.

On the other hand, handstands, scales, and other balanced positions on the beam require a moment of control, which means that the center of gravity must fall within the base of support. From there on, the body will move into a slightly off-balance position in order to facilitate getting into the next move. Positions with a high center of gravity and small base of support (e.g., scale held high on the half-toe or one-handed handstand) are difficult to execute and usually rated higher on the gymnastics difficulty scale.

Pendulum and Beat Swings
PENDULUM SWING

In a pendulum swing, the body moves as one unit, usually in a long hang position. The center of rotation is the object one hangs from, and the center of gravity (the hips) acts like the weight of the pendulum.

There is an acceleration on the way down and a

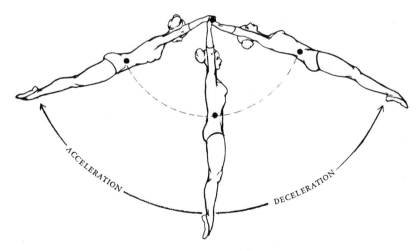

ACCELERATION

DECELERATION

4.2 Pendulum Swing

deceleration (negative acceleration) on the way up, followed by a short period of relative weightlessness at the end of each swing in which the negative acceleration equals the body weight. Many position changes and regrasps or grip changes are performed just prior to or during this moment of relative weightlessness in uneven bar work. It is also important to note that the higher the center of gravity of the pendulum is lifted or placed on one end of the swing, the higher it will ride on the other end. This is especially important in uneven bar skills requiring long, swinging actions.

BEAT SWING

In a beat swing, the body is alternately piked and arched (while it is in a hanging position below the bar) in order to create the moment of relative weightlessness during which desired changes in body position can be made. The natural flexibility of the bar itself is utilized here in order to help with this effect. The beat swing principle can be seen in work in drop kip moves on the uneven bars. For a beginner, it can be useful in executing pullovers to the top bar from a long hang and other similar position changes.

Rotational Movements

Rotation means movement of a body around a fixed point called the axis.

In each rotational movement, the body revolves around one or two of these axes. An axis can be an object (the bar around which one rotates) or a point within the body (as when one performs a somersault). Likewise it can be stationary (bar) or it can move with the body (somersault). Rotation along the longitudinal axis is also called twisting.

The velocity of a body rotating around a fixed point is determined by the length of the radius of rotation, among other things. With a given angular momentum, the longer the radius of rotation, the slower the rotation. The shorter the radius of rotation, the faster the rotation. The radius of rotation itself is defined as the distance between the center of gravity of the rotating body and the center of rotation or axis around which it rotates.

This principle can most easily be seen in rotating moves around uneven bars, and especially in moves starting from and ending in a support position on the same bar. In the execution of a forward split circle,

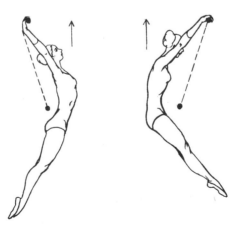

4.3   Beat Swing

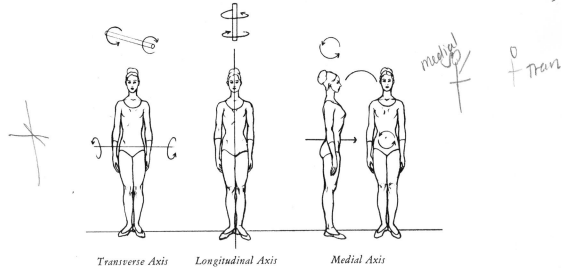

Transverse Axis   Longitudinal Axis   Medial Axis

4.4   Main Axes of the Human Body

for example, during the first half of the circle the body should be elongated and the center of gravity lifted off the bar in order to let the gravity act upon a long lever and create more angular momentum. During the second half of the circle, with gravity acting against the direction of rotation, the radius of rotation should be shortened (by pulling the bar back into contact with the crotch), thus increasing the rotation in order to return to the support position.

Newton's Laws of Motion
LAW OF INERTIA
Masses in motion tend to stay in motion and masses at rest tend to stay at rest unless acted upon by an outside force.

The fact that masses in motion tend to stay in motion is very important in understanding the blocking action in aerial tumbling and vaulting. A runner in motion, moving horizontally, will stay on the horizontal path unless she helps to create a vertical force to partially redirect the horizontal movement and take

her up into the air. In order to do this, she must reach forward with the legs prior to her last contact with the floor and exert a strong push in the forward-downward direction. This is called blocking. As a result, her center of gravity will rise at a predetermined angle. The direction and size of this angle will depend upon the forces involved and the angle at which they are applied.

As mentioned before, this blocking action is very important in obtaining lightness and height in aerial tumbling. (Some of its many applications can be seen in Figure 4.6.)

In a front handspring, the performer should reach forward with both hands prior to contacting the floor and then exert a strong push with her arms in the forward-downward direction (against the floor) as her legs kick up into the handspring. In a front aerial, the last step forward in the hurdle should exert a push in the forward-downward direction, and the performer should definitely reach forward with her lead leg in order to achieve a correct pushing angle. The landing position after a round-off prior to executing a back

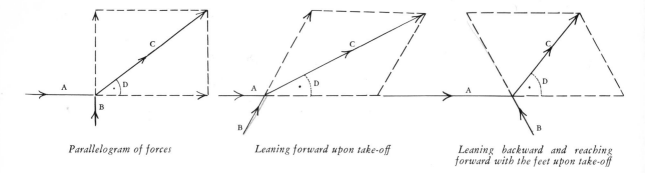

Parallelogram of forces   *Leaning forward upon take-off*   *Leaning backward and reaching forward with the feet upon take-off*

4.5   Examples of the Angle of Rise of the Center of Gravity with Vertical Force (Push) Applied at Different Angles

A.   Horizontal force (run).

B.   Vertical force (reaction to the downward push with legs).

C.   Resultant, path of the center of gravity.

D.   Angle of rise of the center of gravity of the gymnast.

somersault differs from the landing position prior to a back handspring. The back somersault requires that more of the forward momentum be redirected upward. Therefore, the performer should reach back with both legs and execute the final push in the forward-downward direction in relation to the direction of travel. She is reaching out behind her with both legs in order to push into the somersault.

LAW OF ACCELERATION

When the body is acted upon by a force, the resulting bodily acceleration is proportional to the force involved and inversely proportional to the mass of the body.

A girl vaulting over a horse and giving an additional push to her already moving body by pushing off the horse with her hands is applying this principle. The stronger the push and the lighter the girl, the more effect this application of additional force will have on the trajectory of her afterflight. This law also has applications on uneven parallel bars, in moves where an additional push or pull with the arms against the bar (while the body is in motion) is needed for the completion of the stunt.

LAW OF ACTION-REACTION

For every action, there is an equal and opposite reaction. This law applies to almost every move we make. Disregarding friction, we could not walk forward if we did not have a solid floor to push against. (For example, try running in a deep sandpile.) We "push the ground down" in order to leap up. Since the ground is stationary, we move in the direction opposite the push. Likewise, a gymnast pushes away from the bars in order to execute a cast. The bars are relatively stationary, so the gymnast moves. Newton's third law is also the other important factor in understanding blocking and parallelogram of forces. The last contact with the ground in a blocking action in tumbling should be a push which results in a force opposite to the direction in which the push was exerted.

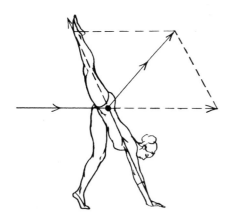

Reaching forward upon hand contact, blocking in a front handspring.

Result: Light, high handspring.

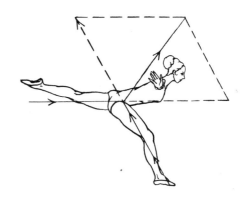

Stepping out and pushing in a forward-down direction, shoulders directly over (not in front of) the pushing foot; blocking in an aerial.

Result: Light, high aerial.

Landing from a round-off in preparation for a back handspring.

Notice the off-balance position and the lack of blocking action, since backward momentum is needed.

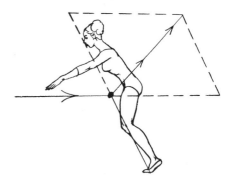

Landing from a round-off prior to a back somersault. Notice the backward reach with legs and the blocking action, since upward momentum is needed.

4.6   Applications of Blocking Action in Tumbling

TECHNICAL ANALYSIS OF SELECTED TUMBLING AND ACROBATIC STUNTS

Good Technique	Common Technical Errors	Results

Backward Extension Roll

Clean, effortless execution going right up to handstand under control.

Extending too early.

Extending too late.

toes to ceiling??

Falling backward arching out of it.

Body raises on an angle, not straight up.

Weak or mistimed extension.

Bent elbows.

Roll too slow.

Show of effort in getting up.

Power

Handstand

Good body alignment (no arch); effortless kick into a controlled position; easy to combine with other skills.

relax arms

Back arched; abdomen relaxed.

Unattractive; hard to control or combine with other skills.

Head up too high.

Unattractive; back forced into arch.

full split.   *full bridge*

Start	Good	Poor

4.7   Front Walkover

Start   With full body extension.
Good   Arch in the upper back.
Poor   Arch in lower back; shoulders are falling forward.

NO POP

Front Walkover

Controlled execution (arching the upper back); complete split in the inverted position; ability to come out with one leg held high off the ground. The shoulders should stay

Use of the lower back instead of the upper back.

Jerky execution.
Heavy landing.
Bent knee landing.
Lack of control.
Unattractive.

Good Technique	Common Technical Errors	Results

over the hands and not move forward as the body arches over.

Chin on chest; rounded upper back.

Possible lower back injury.

No arch.
Collapse on landing.

4.8   Back Walkover

Start   With one leg held up high, lift up the ribcage.
Arch   In upper back for a smooth weight transfer. Pinch shoulder blades together for a better upper back arch.
Stretch   In inverted position, lift the hips and ribcage, stretch at the shoulders.
Land   Under control, head in line with the body, push with hands.

Back Walkover

Ability to go into it with one leg up in front; smooth execution, with no noticeable kick, jerk, or lift in order to get over; no sagging at the shoulders in the inverted position (complete body extension); ability to stretch into a full split in the inverted support; and ability to control the speed of the walkover, stopping in different positions if necessary. The move should start with a lifting action in the ribcage area before any backward bending is attempted. This lift should be followed with a pulling together of the shoulder blades and a strong upper back arch.

Use of the lower back instead of the upper back.

Getting "stuck."
Heavy landing.
Bent knee pullover.
Unattractive.
Lack of control.
Possible lower back injury.

No shoulder nor upper back stretch in the inverted position.

Unattractive.
Too fast.
Cannot be combined with other stunts.
Bent knee pullover.

Good Technique	Common Technical Errors	Results

Round-off

No loss of speed during the execution of the stunt; quick twist and snap-down into an off-balance position; hands contact the mat in quick succession, (with fingers facing back toward the starting point) and a vigorous shoulder push is exerted as the body weight passes over them; the head does *not* lead, but stays in line with the body. The most common mistake is twisting the shoulders too early. The entire approach should be similar to that of the handspring (not the cartwheel) until the hands are about to touch the ground. At that point, a vigorous shoulder twist is executed.

Insufficient speed.
Leaning back in the hurdle on take-off.
Starting the twist too early.
Poor hand position for pushing off; fingers are facing forward in the direction of travel.
No snap-down action.
Head stays down, instead of looking up and ahead upon landing.

All these result in a "dead" round-off, no backward speed, and a poor landing position (shoulders in front of hips).

Poor   *Good*

4.9   Landing Positions Out of Round-off

Poor   Head down, shoulders in front of hips. Will result in a "whip back" somie or back handspring.

Good   Landing position for a back handspring. Head up, shoulders over hips, body off balance.

Landing position for back somersaults. Head up, body erect, feet reaching back.

Front Handspring

Straight body approach, reaching forward with both hands; long step forward and straight leg kick-

Insufficient speed in running.
Kick and push with legs too weak.
Poor body position in the hurdle

Stalling halfway through the handspring, resulting in a squat landing or rotation around one arm.

Good Technique	Common Technical Errors	Results

ing up in back; blocking action with hands and body; pushing off of hands with noticeable rise off the floor; soft landing with the weight over the balls of the feet. The most common mistake is tucking the legs halfway through the handspring and not keeping the body stretched until landing.

(not stretched enough), resulting in lack of speed.

Tucking the head.
Bending the elbows.
Bent knee kick-up.
Hurdle step too short.
Legs kicking up bent over head instead of straight up in back.
Not looking at the mat until hands have pushed off.

Rotation too fast.
Too low and extremely unattractive handspring.
Low squat or very arched landing.

Not reaching out with the arms before contacting the floor with hands.

Low handspring with shoulders in front of hands in the inverted support position.

Not pushing in the inverted position as center of gravity passes over the hands (timing the push wrongly).

Landing with weight over the heels.
No "rising" action off the hands.

Back Handspring

Starting in an off-balance position; head, arms and upper body moving as a unit (head *not* in the lead); hips extended until hands contact floor; finishing in an off-balance position (if more than one is executed in a row); each handspring faster than the previous one; lightness and speed of execution. The most common mistake is throwing the head back first instead of following the hands with the eyes and not moving the head until arms move up past it.

Taking off from a balanced position with weight over the balls of the feet.

Too high, floating back handspring.

Not sitting back straight (leaning too far back).

Flat back handspring; lack of time to rotate properly.

Throwing the head back first (could be caused by an in-balance take-off position).

Low, whip-back style back handspring.
Collapsed landing on bent arms; "froggy" style, with bent knees and legs apart.

Not extending the hips upon take-off.

Piking or tucking during the flight.

Good Technique	Common Technical Errors	Results
	Pulling the knees over (could be the result of being in balance during take-off and therefore afraid of lack of rotation).	"Froggy." Not passing through a handstand position. Feet on the way down by the time the hands contact the floor. Timing off. Lack of control.

arms by ears ALL

Poor

Good

4.10   Back Handspring

Poor   Head is thrown back first; knees are in the lead.

Bent arms and knees in the inverted position, shoulders in front of hands.

Head down, shoulders forward, heavy landing; hard to combine with other stunts.

Good   Head stays in between the arms, hips in lead.

Vertical position upon hand contact, shoulders over hands.

Snapping down with feet, pushing off with hands, head in line with body.

Good Technique	*Common Technical Errors*	*Results*

4.11   Take-off Positions for Front Aerial

Poor Body weight in front of the pushing foot, no blocking action, arms ready to whip downward.

Poor Upper body thrown down, body below horizontal, arms held next to the body.

Good Reaching out and blocking, upper body horizontal, arms whip out to the sides as the support leg pushes off.

Aerials (Front and Side)

Using only two or three running steps; stepping out and blocking upon take-off; completely extending both legs; not leaning down past the horizontal; lifting with arms and upper body during the aerial. The whole body seems to rise during its rotation and be momentarily suspended in the air. Soft landing. Relaxed use of arms, with legs doing all the work. Most common mistakes are:

1. Throwing head and arms downward.
2. Pushing with the leg too late.
3. Leaning too far forward on take-off.

Too many running steps in preparation of the stunt.

Leaning too far down into the aerial (forward or sidewise).

Throwing the arms and upper body downward instead of leaning forward and then lifting up with the arms.

Not "blocking" upon take-off.

Poorly directed kick with the back leg.

Tucking the head and rounding the upper back.

Taking off a straight leg, using ankle push only (knee should be slightly bent, then push).

Not stepping out far enough.

Weight in front of pushing leg.

Not fully extending the pushing leg before taking off.

Low, heavy aerial, barely getting around.

Good Technique	*Common Technical Errors*	*Results*

Tuck Back Somersault

"Blocking" out of the round-off; reaching up with arms; lifting chest and hips up in front of the body, not using the head until the last minute (during the second half of the move). Good tuck position in the air. The whole move goes up, instead of back. Light, bouncy landing. Most common mistakes are not using the arms to reach up with and throwing head back first.

Not reaching up with arms.
Throwing the head back first.
Not "blocking" the take-off.

Not lifting the chest and hips up in front.
Not pulling the knees up at the end of the reach.

Low, whip-back style; loosely tucked somersault.

Insufficient rotation.
Stalling.
Loose tuck.
Rotation too slow.

Poor

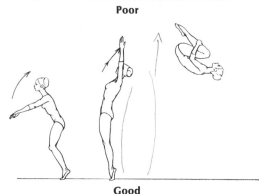

Good

4.12   Tuck Back Somersault

Poor   No blocking action. Head is thrown back first, lack of full body extension before leaving the ground. Result: Low, whip-back type somersault; loose tuck.

Good   Blocking the take-off, arms and chest reach up, head stays between the arms until the knees are tucked.

4.13   Layout Back Somersault

Good Blocking on take-off, reaching up with the arms, head in line with the body, hips and chest lifting up in front, full body extension.

Layout position in the air, head looking for the landing spot, hips in the lead, rotation completed before landing.

Layout Back Somersault

"Blocking" out of the round-off; reaching up with the arms; lifting the chest and hips even more than in a tuck-back somersault. Head stays in line with the body. Move goes up instead of back. Complete rotation before landing; no need to pike down.

Poor, whip-back style head and arm action.
Not lifting the chest and hips.
Poor "block."
Not extending the body and legs upon take-off.
Throwing upper body back instead of lifting chest and hips up in front.

Low layout.
Insufficient time for complete rotation.
Heavy landing.
Piking or tucking on the way down in order to get the feet under.
Bent knee or piked body execution.

Good Technique	*Common Technical Errors*	*Results*

Back Full Twisting Somersault

All the requirements for a good back layout, plus twisting early (the twist should be completed between 10 and 2 o'clock) in order to facilitate a good landing.

Whip-back style head and arm action.
Twisting right off the ground without reaching up first.

Low twister.
Hard to complete the twist.
Low and heavy landing unsafe.
Extremely unattractive.

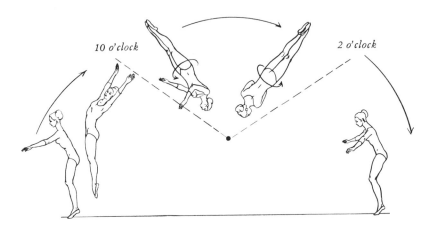

4.14 Back Full Twisting Somersault

Good Blocking the take-off, full body extension and reaching with arms, head in line with the body, slight twist initiated off the ground.

Arm thrown across the chest to increase rotation, both arms close to body, twist executed between 10 and 2 o'clock, straight body rotation completed before landing.

5

*Dance in Gymnastics**

CAROLYN OSBORN BOWERS

INTRODUCTION

The fundamentals of dance technique are utilized as the basis for routine composition in balance beam and floor exercise. The gymnast integrates ballet, jazz, modern dance, and folk dance movements with tumbling and acrobatics in appropriate gymnastic combinations.

The gymnast is expected to perform with perfect technique, yet her dance movements may differ from those of the dance source in order that she may freely integrate them in gymnastic style. She should avoid sprinkling single unrelated skills randomly throughout the design of a routine. On the other hand, there must be no sloppy technique in the name of gymnastic combination. Each gymnast, therefore, must choose carefully those types of movements which she will be capable of performing together. She must not look like a jazz dancer, then a tumbler, and then a ballerina as she performs her routine.

There has been a paradox in the use of dance with other elements in gymnastic routines. The number of creative combinations possible is infinite, but this has not insured originality. The gymnast has great freedom for creativity in movement, yet on the whole gymnastics has used only a select group of dance movements which integrate tastefully and appropriately. As her level of ability increases, the gymnast should be increasingly creative within the design of a gymnastic routine. Greater body control allows for more success in transitions and combinations. The coach also must work for a creative rather than imitative style in each developing gymnast. The encouragement of creativity is a very difficult task when there are so many fundamentals to be learned.

The selection of dance movements for an exercise is determined in part by the gymnast's ability to execute them within a complete routine. Some of the factors involved are endurance, the goals of composition discussed in the balance beam and floor exercise chapters, and maximum amplitude in execution. Gymnastics is rapidly reaching a level in the United States where sound technical ability is only the *first* prerequisite for national prominence. The *second* prerequisite is a unique and personal style. All movements, whether large or small, must appear to have a purpose within the design and the music chosen. Flair and excitement are brought to the routine by the unusual modification of dance movements. Yet the gymnast must study each section of the complete routine to insure that she has not violated the principles involved in the correct execution of leaps, turns, and balances and has not lost the elegance of good body line.

*The author wishes to express her appreciation to Mrs. Margaret Patton, Assistant Professor of Dance at The Ohio State University, for her helpful suggestions.

TECHNICAL ANALYSIS OF SELECTED DANCE MOVEMENTS

Criteria for Selection and Format

The dance movements to be analyzed in this section are of the following kinds:

1. Dance movements which find their source in the technique of classical ballet.
2. Dance movements frequently used in current gymnastic performances.
3. Leaps, turns, and balances.
4. Medium and superior difficulties (in balance beam and floor exercise) which originate from dance movements.

Each section includes a description of good technique as viewed by the judge. This description is not designed for basic instruction but to emphasize amplitude and correct technical execution. A list of common technical errors and their effect on performance follows each description. Those skills related to ballet technique are described first as they originate in pure ballet and then as they are adapted for gymnastics use.

Posture

BASIC STANDING POSTURE

Good Technique	Common Technical Errors	Results
A plumb line dropped from the ear lobe would dissect the midpoint of the shoulder and hip and fall behind the patella and in front of the lateral malleolus. The head is held erect, chest lifted, and shoulders relaxed. Abdominal muscles are tight, with total control from shoulders to hips. The back is straight and the hips are tucked under.	Lordosis (an extreme swayback often found in young gymnasts), due to a lack of abdominal muscular development and tightening of the muscles in the lower back.	Gymnast may assume poses with this body line. Contorted appearance. Lack of elegance and extension.
	Protruding abdomen, due to lack of muscular conditioning or to overweight.	Poor body line. Gymnast appears tired and is unable to lift body as unit for leaps and turns.
	Head strained too far upward or thrown past natural level of chin.	Appears affected. Lacks control; poor space orientation. Poor continuity; lack of ease in performance.
	Head forward (cause may or may not be postural); shoulders rounded; rearward thrust of hips, protruding abdomen.	Poor body line. Body unable to achieve graceful extension of movement. Balance movements difficult. Turns off balance.
	Abdomen and back stiff; shoulders lifted and strained.	Incorrect force for leaps. Lack of ease and suppleness. Awkward appearance.

Poor

Preparation Not enough demi-plié. Head and body forward. Entire foot not pushing into floor.

Take-off Working leg thrust weak, with knee bent. Body losing back control.

Leap Arms flying, shoulders lifted. Front leg too high for lift of rear leg. Poor turnout of rear leg. Landing will be on heel with weight back.

Good

Preparation Body over support leg with upright posture. Entire foot on floor. Good demi-plié.

Take-off Last push from toes. Working leg stretched to lift. Back extended in control. Torso extended. Body moves as unit with legs. Shoulders relaxed.

Leap Rear leg turned out with lift equal to front leg. Good split, knees stretched. Shoulders relaxed.

Landing Gymnast has landed toe-heel, with weight balanced over landing leg to allow for soft demi-plié. Rear leg straight back (not swinging to side).

5.1 Split Leap

POSTURE IN GYMNASTICS

Basic standing posture as described above places the body segments in line, one above the other, with the weight equally balanced over the base of support. Since all gymnastic performance is a matter of balance, control of forces, and timing, the application of good posture is fundamental to both execution and appearance.

For example, the body position is critical in achieving high leaps which have soft controlled landings. The gymnast must be able to hold her torso straight with the muscles pulled in, the chest lifted, the head balanced gracefully, and the shoulders relaxed. Posture should be natural, even though it is achieved through conscious effort. It should not be stiff and strained. The gymnast must also be able to control the angle and placement of the torso so as to achieve balance over the landing leg. (See figure 5-1)

A second example of the importance of posture is seen in the pirouette, figure 5-2. The base of support becomes smaller and a turning force is applied to the body.

Poor

Preparation Poor movement into turn initiated by too much arm and shoulder thrust, pulling body off turning axis. Hip position is open and free leg is sideward to offset initial movement.

Turning Posture, Side View Weight slightly back, with hips counterbalancing by extending forward. Spin will pull body farther off base of support. Heel will lower to save balance or cause incomplete turn.

Turning Posture, Front View Turn without torso control. Shoulders pulling body out of line with supporting foot. Fall or step on other foot necessary.

Good

Preparation From a lunge (by choice): gymnast will perform demi-plié and transfer weight to forward foot while arms and torso initiate turn.

Turning Posture, Side View Body lifts up over base of support (half-toe). Slight forward lean, chest lifted, abdomen pulled in. Turn around axis, with weight balanced over base.

Turning Posture, Front View Body balanced directly over base of support (half-toe). Slight forward lean, toes gripping floor.

5.2 Pirouette

The position in which the muscles hold the body segments influences whether the spin rotates around the vertical axis or pulls the body mass off balance with incomplete execution.

Relationship of Gymnastic Dance to Ballet
DEFINITIONS

Beat: a beat is executed in the lower leg at the calf. The legs are brought together in a tight fifth position. A beat is accomplished by standing in the fifth position (see figure 5-7), jumping straight into the air, pulling the legs tightly together, and returning to the fifth position.

Demi-plié: the heels remain in contact with the floor, the ankles bend, and the knees bend, moving forward over the toes. There is flexion at the hips, but the torso remains in an upright posture.

Elancer: to dart.

Etendre: to stretch.

Extension: The carriage of the body segments so that they are lifted or stretched to be balanced correctly with a controlled body line. The term extension may be used to correct a sagging posture or a leg position which is not held tightly enough at the knee for straight perfection. Extension may also be used to describe flexibility and muscle control in holding a high leg position, generally to the side or rear and turned out.

Glisser: to glide or slide. A common movement is the glissade.

Plier: to bend. A common movement is the plie.

Positions of the feet and arms: see figures 5-3 through 5-7. Although there are regulations against beginning and finishing with classic ballet positions of the feet and arms, there is value in some knowledge and use of these positions in the study of posture and in coordinating movements of the body with those of the arms and legs.

Relever: to raise. A common movement is the relevé.

Sauter: to jump. A common movement is the sauté (or, if combined with other terms, the saut).

Support leg: the leg which supports the body during a movement or in a static position. Also, the leg which leaves the floor last for a leap or hop.

Tourner: to turn around.

Turnout: a rotation of the leg at the hip for better body line. For example, in the arabesque (see 5.8), the support leg faces forward and the working leg is raised directly to the rear with the side of the leg toward the ceiling and the knee at right angles to the support leg knee.

Working leg (or gesture leg): the leg which thrusts, raises, or slides into a dance movement or position.

5.3   First Position

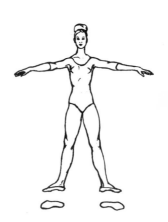

5.4   Second Position

5.5   Third Position

5.6   Fourth Position

5.7   Fifth Position

Good Technique	*Common Technical Errors*	*Results*

Arabesque

Each school of ballet has several arabesque positions. All are in profile with support on one leg (straight or bent in demi-plié). The working leg is extended rearward; the shoulders are square to the direction faced; and the arm positions create the longest line possible from fingers to toes. Gymnastics allows more freedom in the position. It will not always be in profile, arms and legs may be bent and twisted, and the body may twist. When an arabasque is executed in an extended manner, the gymnast should strive to raise the rearward leg to a right angle to the support leg, as in ballet.

Working leg not held high enough to be rearward at right angles to support leg.

Insufficient amplitude.

Working leg loose at knee.

Form break.

No leg turnout at hip. Knee turned under.

Poor body line.
Lack of amplitude.

Twisted body line or bent leg not definite in design.

Sloppy technique.
Lack of meaning in composition.

Poor

Good

Poor   Working leg too low; loss of arch in body line.

Good   Toes grip floor, with slight lean forward on support leg.
Working leg raised at least to right angle to support leg.
Body line arched.

5.8   Arabesque

Good Technique	*Common Technical Errors*	*Results*

Arabesque Penchée: Front Scale (Deep Scale)

The upper body is lowered while the working leg is raised higher. The foot of the working leg must be the highest point. Legs are turned out. A long arched body line which is obliquely downward is demonstrated.

Upper body lowered further than working leg able to raise.
Late elevation of working leg.

Knees not stretched fully when intended to be straight.

Body line destroyed, buttocks prominent.
Lack of elegance.
Lack of continuity.

Form break (generally small to medium deduction).

Arabesque Penchée: Needle Scale

The working leg continues to raise until it is extended in a perfect split. The upper body may be slightly arched or may move briefly to a position against the support leg.

Upper body reaches for support leg too soon.
Slow movement to split.
Lack of control in split position.
Lowering of extended leg too soon.

Lack of stretch in support leg; weight on heel rather than forward on toes.

Poor body line.
Awkward movement.
Lack of continuity.
Insufficient amplitude.

Split incomplete.

Attitude

One leg supports. The working (or gesture) leg must be extended directly back and is well turned out; the lower leg is bent (90-degree angle at knee) and carried horizontally. The position may be learned from a proper arabesque with the knee held high as the lower leg is bent. The knee must be higher than the foot. The arm on the support leg side is extended out to the side. The other arm is curved overhead. Gymnastics allows free arm variation.

Poor posture.

Knee below foot level.
Leg not lifted high enough in back.

Leg not lifted directly to rear.

Lack of elegance.

Poor form (small to medium errors).

Opens to side: awkward.
Poor body line.

Good Technique	Common Technical Errors	Results

Assemblé

A jump from one support to two; it is executed to the side, front, or rear, or with a turn. The working leg may execute a low slide or sweep high into the air as a grande battement. As the working leg brushes, push off floor by support leg and toes. The viewer should see distinctly: (a) the working leg extended in the air and (b) both legs closing together before landing. Legs land simultaneously in fifth position. Land softly toe, heel, demi-plié.

Movement not clearly executed.
Elevation insufficient.
Landing not preceded by definite closing of legs.

Poor quality; affects appearance and style.
Performer not in air as working leg is out.
Lack of distinctive movement in composition.
Poor technique.

Stiff and jerky landing.

Lack of lightness and suppleness.

Entrechat

A jump into the air. Posture is upright, with a rapid beat (see definitions) of the legs in the air as they change places front to back. The movement is progressively more difficult with a greater number of beats. (The difficulty rating on balance beam increases with a greater number of beats.)

The simple exchange of foot position is called changement (fifth position right foot front to fifth position right foot back). If the performer jumps to a tight beat from the starting position and then changes to land, the movement is designated as changement royal.

Entrechats are further designated by the number of beats counted beyond the changement. When the

Beats are not definite or completed.

Off balance.
Stiff landing.
Lack of continuity with following movement.

Torso movement.
Twisting of the hips during beats.

Poor body line.
Poor timing.
Off balance.

Good Technique	*Common Technical Errors*	*Results*
performer jumps, exchanges the leg position, and returns the legs to land (the beats are counted as three if landing on one foot and four if landing with the feet together) in fifth position as begun, the movement is called entrechat quatre. Each additional exchange in the air adds numerically to the number of beats (odd numbers for landing on one foot and even numbers landing feet together).		

Chassé

One foot chases the other and replaces its position. The feet do not pass each other as in a run. It is executed in the air not unlike a gallop.	Legs loose, not extended.	Form break; sloppy definition in movement.
Step out to push off front foot. The legs come together in the air. The rear foot lands first, displacing the front foot. Ballet designates the chassé to the front, side, and rear. Gymnastics usually designates the chassé to the front and uses the terms "slide" and "gallop" for movements to the side and rear, respectively.	Legs not brought together. Movement too low. Arm movements not coordinated with footwork.	Movement is technically not completed. Lack of rhythm and coordination.

Jeté (Leap)

The leg positions for the jeté and grand jeté, the body positions, and the focus may be much more creative in gymnastics than in ballet. The legs may show a strong bend at the knees and may even extend to a second position before landing, depending upon the skill of the performer. The body may twist or arch and the arms may be placed asymmetrically. The only requirement is that the gymnast be able to move into a position for balanced posture in a soft landing.

The gymnast may also utilize one-quarter turns to full turns or more during the leap. The landing may move directly to the floor or into another gymnastic element.

Good Technique	Common Technical Errors	Results
The jeté is executed from one leg to the other. The working leg is swung and thrust forcefully into the air. The preparation of the support leg is demi-plié with the entire foot placed on the floor. Power for the leap comes from the thrust against the floor resulting from leg and ankle extension and the final pushoff of the toes.	Working leg not thrust high enough. Landing without demi-plié. Back loses control and stability.	Lack of amplitude. Less brilliance in execution. Stiff and heavy. Lack of definition. Sloppy design.

Grand Jeté en Avant (Large Jeté Forward, or Split Leap)

Usually preceded by a run or slide for needed force. The height of the leap is determined by (a) direction (upward) of working leg and (b) the strength of the support leg thrust. Length of travel depends upon the push from the support leg. The support leg must be thrust up and back to equal the height of the lead leg. The body rises as a unit, seems to float in the air, and descends to the ground in the same pose, landing in a soft demi-plié, the back leg still extended. The split leap must be demonstrated with maximum amplitude in split, balance, and light landing. (See figure 5-1.)	Lack of strength in execution. Back loses control and stability. Working leg lifted too high for ability of gymnast. Legs not stretched. Strain in shoulders. Lack of strong leg thrust. Shoulders collapse forward. Landing without demi-plié. Weight backward.	Low height (rear leg may not equal height of front leg). Note: The height of the leap cannot be compared between gymnasts because of structural differences. Poor timing. Lack of definition. Landing off balance and hard. Lack of equal leg split; not balanced. Jerky. Poor form. Stiffness. Lack of suppleness. Insufficient amplitude. Inelegance. Not floating in air. Heavy landing. Loss of balance and body position.

Poor

Preparation   Moving into tour jeté.

Body Position   Body turning too soon while support leg is still contacting floor. Loss of height in leap and excitement in execution.

Timing   Legs do not come together. Working leg makes descent as support leg rises. Body cannot lift higher because legs are working against each other.

Landing   Off balance, as torso is too far forward. Loss of arch and good arabesque position. Heavy landing.

Good

Preparation   Executed from a series of slides. Body is in motion, will be in balance over support leg for strong thrust, and is turning into the take-off direction.

Body Position before Turn   Working leg thrust up. Support leg has extended forcefully, pushing into the floor, and is brought up to working leg.

Timing of Turn   Turn is executed when legs meet and must be rapid. Working leg will reach for floor. Arms have swept upward. Overhead position is one which will aid turn.

Landing   Support leg is now held in arabesque. Arms move to desired placement. Torso over landing leg, arabesque posture. Land toe-heel, demi-plié.

5.9   Jeté en Tournant (Tour Jeté)

Good Technique	Common Technical Errors	Results

Jeté en Tournant (Tour Jeté)

Usually preceded by slides or a run. The working leg is thrust into the air, the turn (half) is made in mid-air, and the legs pass close to each other (knees extended). The back is arched. The landing is toe-heel in a demi-plié facing the direction from which the body comes. The timing involves an upward thrust of the leg. The support leg pushes to close the legs together. Then the turn is made quickly as the working leg lands (demi-plié). Landing position is an arabesque. Gymnasts should execute the leap with correct technique but will not necessarily hold the arabesque finish. The gymnast will show a good arabesque posture but may move into a needle scale or drop the leg into a take-off for another gymnastic element.

Lack of height.

Shoulders raised to help lift the body.
Early rotation.
Turn not made while entire body is in air.

Turn made before support leg is in air.

Legs do not pass in air; stiff and heavy landing.

Low leap.
Strained, not elegant.
No suspended feeling.
Body leans too far forward to maintain arch.
Off balance.
Not a leap.

Pas de Chat or Saut de Chat (Cat Leap or Cat Jump)

The ballet description is that of a jump from and return to fifth position, in which the back foot (working leg) is brought upward with the knee bending sharply and legs turned out. As the support leg (front foot) pushes to jump upward, it replaces the back, with both legs bent under the body in the air. The rear foot lands, followed by the front foot. The movement often is sidewards.

Lack of strength in leg thrust.
Weak push off floor, poor preparatory plié.

Poor turnout.
Poor posture.

Lack of timing in passing of legs.
No demi-plié.

Insufficient amplitude.
Low jump.

Form breaks.

Lack of rhythm.
Heavy landing.
Lack of continuity with following movement.

Good Technique	*Common Technical Errors*	*Results*

Gymnastics has a modified movement for the pas de chat. The working leg swings forward and up in a half-bent, turned-out position. The jump is made from the support leg and it also swings forward and up to pass the descending working leg. The legs follow each other in landing demi-plié. Often the accompanying arm movement sweeps forward and upward. On the balance beam the movement is always carried forward and it usually is a forward motion on the floor.

Preparation   Step into demi-plié. Working leg sweeps from behind, knee leads, and leg is turned out as foot passes support leg.

Take-off   Support leg extends and pushes forcefully into floor. Working leg and arms sweep upward.

Leap   Body is propelled upward, and the support leg is brought up to the working leg, which is starting descent. Both legs are turned out.

Landing   Body is inclined slightly forward over landing leg, landing toe-heel, demi-plié. Free leg is high, moving to take a step.

5.10   Pas de Chat (Cat Leap)

Tour (Turn or Spin)

The body turns, with support on the ground unless specified "en l'air." Turns are executed by rotation about an axis for balance. They must be on half-toe to the	Executed on flat foot.	Poor balance. Lack of sureness. Lack of strength in execution.
	Failure to turn around axis.	Loss of balance.

Good Technique	Common Technical Errors	Results
finish of the turn. Then the heel is lowered. The turn begins in the body. The performer appears to be lifted: the torso is firm, the body turns as a unit, and the arm and leg positions are assumed gracefully.	Shoulders lift or lead. Torso strained. Loss of control in back; body not turning as a unit. No definite design in arm and free leg positions.	Heavy execution. Stiffness. Lack of rhythm and sureness in turn. Lack of variety in turns. Poor form.

Turn, Support Leg Bent

The support leg must be bent far enough to look definitely designed. Movement out of the bent leg position must also be exact. Execution is on half-toe. Free leg may be designed in any position.	As listed for tour. Body bends too much. Shoulders lead. Movement not initiated in torso.	As listed for tour. Awkward body line. Loss of balance. Gymnast is unable to remain on half-toe to finish of turn.

Preparation Stepping into wide lunge with arms reaching to side for preparation of horizontal sweep.

Beginning of Turn With weight over ball of foot, torso moves down and sideward at same time. Working leg rises strongly to lead into scale. Support leg straightens as arched balance position is established.

Turning Position Body balanced over ball of foot. Rotation continues. Torso holds controlled arch position.

Finish Torso will rise first, keeping good arabesque position. Balance is still held over ball of foot.

5.11 Turn in Arabesque Penchée (Front Scale)

Turn in Arabesque Penchée (Front Scale)

The turn is executed in a deep-scale position. The body must	As listed for turns.	As listed for turns.

Good Technique	Common Technical Errors	Results
move into the deep scale (see arabesque penchée) as the force is initiated from torso movement and from the preparatory movement (often a large lunge step with a horizontal arm swing). This turn must also be on half-toe, although the heel will be slightly lower than it is for an upright turn.	Break in arch of scale. Leg raised late. Leg not raised sufficiently.	Poor form. Turn incomplete. Loss of balance. Poor body line.
	Turn not initiated in torso. Shoulders thrown out of line from turning axis.	Loss of balance.
	Weight on heel.	Flat-footed turn.

Pirouette

Good Technique	Common Technical Errors	Results
A full turn on one foot. Performer presses the toes against the floor and has a slightly forward lean. The movement has a rapid spin effect forcefully initiated by the arms. The ballet preparation step is usually a demi-plié. The gymnastics preparatory step may vary.	As listed for turns. Leading with shoulders. Loss of control in torso.	As listed for turns. Loss of balance.

Chainé

Good Technique	Common Technical Errors	Results
A half-turn on each foot. The legs are straight, and the movements are executed on half-toe, usually done in a line. In ballet the line is often in a circular pattern. Gymnastics makes use of this type of turn with a wide variety of arm designs and rhythms, from those of formal ballet to those of jazz.	Turns too slow, with weight not centered over base of support. Lack of good posture. Poor head position.	Lack of continuity between half-turns. Loss of balance; appearance of falling backward. Crooked, waivering steps. Stiffness. Poor focus. Loss of excitement and flair.
	Shoulders lifted and strained. Lack of extension in legs.	Lack of suppleness. Lack of elegance.

Tour en l'Air (Turn in the Air)

Good Technique	Common Technical Errors	Results
As the spring is made into the air, the torso and arms have initiated	Too much twist begun on floor. Upper body leads legs.	Off balance. Heaviness.

Good Technique	Common Technical Errors	Results

the turn. The body must rotate as a total unit with good posture. A full turn from a two-foot spring should "jump upward," rotating about the vertical axis to return to the initial starting place in balance.

Turn initiated completely in shoulder.

Landing in segments; poor timing.

Body tilts in air.
Landing unbalanced.

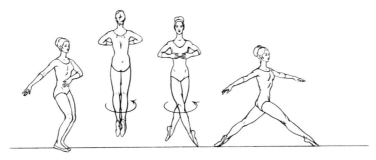

Preparation   Demi-plié; arms will move with torso to initiate spin.

Jump and Turn   Strong leg and ankle extension, straight upward. Arms help to initiate spin and then stop when chest reaches straight posture with hips and legs.

Movement into Split   Arms extend to help stop the rotation. Legs extend equally forward and backward on descent. Rear leg is turned out, with toes reaching for floor. Body balanced in between legs, with slight forward lean of chest over front leg.

Split   Continuous drop to split. Legs push to control the landing of the split.

5.12   Tour en l'Air to Splits

MISCELLANEOUS GYMNASTIC DANCE SKILLS

A few skills have been selected for analysis from those which are often found in current floor exercise and balance beam routines. Because of their established nature in the gymnastic form, these skills have not been related to a parent type of dance.

Barrel Roll Turn

A fast full turn on one foot. The arms chase each other in windmill fashion to provide the force. With

Turn not completed on half-toe.

Poor technique.

Good Technique	*Common Technical Errors*	*Results*

the balance on the right toe, the right arm moves first, starting forward from an overhead position. As it reaches the hips, the body leans slightly to the right, and then straightens. The half-turn is completed when the left arm reaches the hips. The body will lean slightly to the left and then straighten.

Lack of control in finish of turn. Upright posture not regained before next movement.

Lack of continuity. Off balance. Poor timing.

Preparation   Standing left to step onto right half-toe. Body extended upward, hips tucked under, torso tight. Right arm overhead to begin circle.

Start of Turn   Step to balance over half-toe. Upper body leans slightly to right as right arm circles forward and down. Left arm moves upward to chase right arm and help turn.

Half of Turn   As body turns it straightens and right arm pulls up across the chest to overhead. Upper body leans slightly toward left arm as it reaches hips and then straightens again.

Completion of Turn   As turn is completed, body pulls into straight posture over support.

5.13   Barrel Roll Turn

Hitchkick (Scissors Kick)

This may be executed forward or backward. Care must be taken that this movement is not just an easy replacement for a good cabriole. (The ballet cabriole is executed with the support leg beating

General faults of other leaps. (See pages 47 and 49.)

See leaps, pages 47 and 49.

Good Technique	Common Technical Errors	Results
against the working leg to send it back into the air. Landing is on the same support.) The working leg is thrust upwards, the gymnast springs off the support foot to pass legs in the air, and the lead leg lands softly (toe-heel, plié). The second leg should near its highest point when the lead leg lands, to prevent jerky, heavy execution.	Second leg not held in high position when landing.	Heavy landing. Gymnast appears to sink on landing leg.

Knee Spin

The knee spin may be executed on one leg or travel slightly as weight is transferred, one-half turn on each knee. The posture must be upright, with no break at the hips. The spin should move quickly.	Poor posture; body bends at hips in attempt to take weight off knee.	Spin incomplete. Poor rhythm. Lack of continuity. Awkwardness. Off balance.

Pose with Hips Extended

This pose was first used by Caslavska on the balance beam. For lack of better description it is likened to a common pose of Spanish dancers: straight support leg with exaggerated extension at the hip, back arched to counterbalance, arms often held over head, free leg bent, and knees often pressed together. When the pose is utilized with a turn, the turn must end in the balanced position, on half-toe. The gymnast should not be falling into her next step at this point.	Hips not extended forward. Free leg held loosely. Improper counterbalancing of hips and body when turning.	Awkward pose. Lack of amplitude in stretch. Poor body line. Fall out of turn. Turn incomplete. Turn flat-footed.

Good Technique	Common Technical Errors	Results

Scissors Leap

The scissors leap follows the principles of the split leap, except that the legs are switched in mid-air so that the support leg (or take-off foot) is also the landing foot.

The working leg is thrust up and forward. A strong push into the floor is given by the support leg and it thrusts rearward to equal the height of the forward leg (first notable extension). (See jeté.)

The legs are rapidly switched to a full split (second and stronger notable extension), with the height of the two legs in equal balance. The body leans slightly forward in order to be balanced over the landing leg, landing in soft demi-plié.

As listed for jeté and grand jeté en avant.

No rearward leg elevation for first notable jeté extension.

As listed for jeté and grand jeté en avant.

Appearance of a hop with working leg switch. No credit for scissors leap.

Split Jump

A spring from both feet, executed straight into the air, with body slightly inclined forward for balance upon landing. The jump must be high enough to allow time for the legs to reach a full split and come back together before landing toe-heel, demi-plié. The gymnast may move into a squat position upon landing, but this must also be executed softly with continuity.

Unequal and insufficient height of legs.

Legs not extended at knees.

Body twists upon landing (especially on balance beam).

Improper use of foot and demi-plié.

Squat landing; too much bend of legs in air.

Not a true split jump.

Form break.

Body off balance.

Jolt on the landing; heavy.

Heavy landing.

Stag Leap

The stag leap is executed in a manner similar to the jeté. (See page

See general faults of jeté.

As listed for jeté.

Poor

Preparation   Knee lift weak. Poor thrust off support leg.

Stag Position   Working leg held loosely. Back leg not extended or lifted. Shoulders lifted, strained. Poor height.

Open Position   Working leg not fully extended before landing. Back leg not lifted or stretched. Shoulders still strained. Arms not held in any particular design.

Landing   Insufficient amplitude. Next step too rapid. Lack of heel placement and demi-plié. Stiff landing.

Good

Preparation   Strong push from floor and lift from working leg. Shoulders relaxed, arms supple. Torso moves as solid unit over legs.

Stag Position   Legs show stag position with amplitude, forward leg demonstrating a tight flexion, rearward leg turning out and extended. (The focus over the left side by choice and design of competitor.) Arms and shoulders are relaxed.

Open Position   Extension of working leg. Legs raised and stretched equally. May show more amplitude by reaching split.

Landing   Body balanced over landing leg; good posture. Rear leg extended and held until next movement.

5.14   Stag Leap

Good Technique	Common Technical Errors	Results
47.) The difference is that the working leg is thrust up and forward with a sharp bend at the knee. The foot of the working leg momentarily touches the knee of the support leg as the body moves upward off the floor. As the support leg thrusts rearward, the legs stretch in stag position, and then the working leg extends in jeté. The timing will be: lift off floor, stag position, open to jeté, landing. The body may remain in a straight forward position with the hips square to the direction of travel or it may twist to open the hips sideways. In either case the body must be lifted as a unit with the legs to provide for a balanced, soft landing.	Loosely held legs. No extension of bent legs.	Unclear stag position. Insufficient amplitude. Lack of flair in execution. Low leap. Poor form. Poor landing.
	Legs lead body. Loss of torso control.	Heavy landing. Off balance.

Straddle Jump

Executed as the split jump, except that both legs are brought forward and straddled.	Insufficient preparation for lift. Insufficient height.	Incomplete straddle. Insufficient amplitude. Heavy landing.
	Upper body bends to meet legs rather than legs lifting to position parallel to floor.	Loss of balance in landing. Insufficient amplitude. Awkwardness.

DANCE MOVEMENTS AS DIFFICULTIES
Floor Exercise
SUPERIOR DIFFICULTIES

The dance movements which are considered of superior value in floor exercise are combinations of dance skills in which the gymnast must demonstrate great control and timing for perfect execution that has the required continuity. Listed under superior difficulties are:

1. Turning leaps or jumps which rotate more than 360 degrees and finish in a balance, a walkover, or another element.
2. Turning movements (on the balls of the feet) which rotate more than 360 degrees and finish in a balance, a walkover, or another element.

Examples of combinations are:

1. A straight jump into the air, rotating 450 degrees (one and one-fourth turns) and landing in immediate split position.
2. A spring into the air, lifting one leg bent (foot touching other knee) and executing one and one-half turns (540 degrees) to land, bending immediately backwards into a walkover.
3. A jump into the air, bringing legs slightly forward and together, rotating one and one-half turns (540 degrees), and landing in front scale facing the direction opposite from that in which the jump originated.
4. A pirouette of one and one-half turns (540 degrees) in attitude, stopping in immediate deep scale (held to demonstrate balance).

MEDIUM DIFFICULTIES

Most leaps, turning leaps, and turns of 360 degrees or more are listed as medium difficulties. (See chapter VI.) It should be noted that a high degree of amplitude is assumed; all pivots are designated to be on half-toe. A beginner executing an awkward run stag leap which is low and does not show a full stag position with leg extension before landing would probably not receive credit for a medium difficulty.

Balance Beam
SUPERIOR DIFFICULTIES

Many dance movements are considered superior difficulties on the balance beam because of the limitation of the movement surface. Examples are:

1. A full turn in the air from a two-foot take-off.
2. A leap onto one leg, executing an immediate one and one-half turn (free leg in any given position) to finish in a front scale (held to show control).
3. A cat leap turning 180 degrees (half turn) in the air.
4. A rapid gallop (see chassé description) with a half turn in each step-together-step pattern.

MEDIUM DIFFICULTIES

All types of full turns (360 degrees) and jumps with half turns (180 degrees) are considered medium difficulties. Most of the leaps described in the analysis portion of this chapter, such as the stag leap, grand jeté, large cat leap (pas de chat with the legs definitely in front of the body), and a series of leaps and jumps are considered as medium difficulties. For a more complete list refer to the chapter on balance beam.

Evaluating Dance Difficulties

For a judge the line between counting and not counting a difficulty is a fine one. When a turn is completed for the designated number of revolutions on the balance beam, the gymnast usually receives credit for the difficulty and a penalty for the flat foot. In floor exercise, where the technique should be more precise, a medium difficulty would not be awarded for a turn with the foot flat. The gymnast should also begin to show a definite position and some elevation in leaps both on the balance beam and on the floor.

The coach with beginning and intermediate gymnasts would be wise to utilize dance for all important transitions and for variety in composition, rather than for meeting the difficulty requirements. Often the excitement of the meet, fatigue, and lack of endurance for a complete routine will adversely affect the execution of a dance difficulty. The resultant score will be lower than predicted during workouts, in which the difficulties were given their value. The gymnast may thus be consistently disappointed in her performance and become discouraged. The exceptions are those who have been trained in dance and may have excellent control of their movement when they begin gymnastics.

As gymnasts progress to a higher level of ability, they usually develop the strength needed to execute dance movements correctly as difficulties. To achieve a higher score in the routine as one's ability develops provides a psychological boost.

COACHING HINTS TO INCREASE SCORES

Dance movements are so valuable to the total composition in the balance beam and floor exercise events that it is necessary for the coach to spend considerable time improving dance skills. The coach must also work with the gymnast to discover the most effective use for each dance skill.

Assuming the gymnast is just beginning, here are a few hints for coaching:

1. Begin with a basic leap, jump, and turn. Concentrate on the most important principles.
   a. Leaps:
      (1) Force: Bend the leg and ankle for the take-off. Take off from the entire foot. Extend upward with a strong push from the toes. Use a great deal of pushing force downward into the floor to gain a strong lift upward. (Every action has an opposite and equal reaction.)

(2) Arm position: Attempt to find a natural arm position, but do not allow the arms to fly out of control. Do not allow the shoulders to lift and strain with a leap. The shoulders must relax for a graceful and supple appearance. Find and practice one or two basic arm positions with small leaps until the position feels natural. Then use this arm placement when trying to reach full amplitude.

(3) Landing: Emphasize landing on the toe, then placing the heel on the floor, and then bending slightly in demi-plié to soften the landing. The body should be forward over the landing support. The body should have a slight inclination to come up over the take-off foot and to travel with the leap.

(4) Practice: Use two persons on either side of the performer. They support the performer by the arms and help her "feel" the elements of a good leap. The spotters lift as the performer leaps. The performer concentrates upon form, leg position, and the landing. Later in practice the spotters should not lift but may support to delay the landing. The performer should concentrate upon correct soft landing technique. The performer should practice both by herself and with the spotters.

b. Jumps:

(1) Force: When executing a beginning jump a performer should spring off two feet for greater pushing power. A demi-plié or full squat (plié) may be employed in preparation for the jump. The entire foot is again the base for the pushoff, the final thrust coming from the toes.

(2) Arm Position: This should be practiced with the same method used for leaps.

(3) Landing: The same principles as for leaps should be employed.

(4) Practice: A great deal of variety may be found for beginners in jumping. Try many different types of jumps: land on one foot, land on two feet, land and move into a squat, and attempt a variety of arm and leg designs. Choose the jumps which come to the individual performer most easily. Be sure to vary the arm placement. Attempt some of the jumps with a one-fourth or one-half turn. Concentrate upon posture and turning around an axis. Avoid leading too much with the shoulders.

c. Turns:

(1) Experiments: Allow gymnasts to experiment with inward and outward turns. Allow the legs to trail or lead. Choose whichever

type seems to be successful most naturally and work on the finer points of technique with this type first.

(2) Technique: Have the gymnast turn the torso as a whole unit: do not allow a break at the waist in which one half of the body pulls the other half around. Insure that the gymnast presses against the floor with her toes. Do not allow a lift of the shoulders; make the lift come from the chest or center of the body. Concentrate on breathing in as the body lifts to turn. Practice using a full-length mirror to show posture for correct balance. Practice balancing over a half-toe support. Use exercises in which the student attempts half and full turns ending in a half-toe balance in front of the mirror. Spotting with the head may be introduced by having the student focus as long as possible on the mirror and then snap the head around to focus on the mirror for the completion of the turn and balance. Practice turns for the balance beam on a line by having the gymnast spot a focus on an imaginary end of the beam on the floor. Practice turns with a variety of arm positions: hands on hips, one arm up and one down, or both flung out to the side. Design positions for the free leg. Add turns which rotate in the opposite direction and practice on the opposite support leg. In performance (especially on balance beam), use the best turns first.

2. Spend a designated amount of time in each workout session on practice of the basic locomotor movements: walking, a dance run (strong use of legs and feet with large gliding runs, as opposed to knee-lift strides for vaulting), hops, skips, slides in all directions (chassé), grapevine patterns, waltz rhythms, and various combinations of these. Emphasize elegance of movement, posture, different focus and head positions. Practice using the locomotor patterns. Add simple arm patterns after the leg patterns are established. Practice moving from a locomotor pattern into a pose. Practice moving into a simple tumbling skill with no break between the pattern and the skill.

3. Perform exercises in each workout which will emphasize supple body movements (rhythmic swinging movements, bending with locomotion in which the body sweeps downward and returns to extended posture, rotation of the torso with bending combinations, torso movement with different arm patterns).

4. Use movements the gymnast finds easy to perform. Many people assume erroneously that if something is not difficult to learn, it is worthless. Of course, variety in all types of movement is an eventual goal. The beginner

will have more success at an earlier stage if allowed to utilize her natural abilities in her routines. She can then build toward variety. Practice workouts and performances are different. The performer will tend to lose her balance and her concentration in performance when forced to use unnatural combinations.

5. Endurance is as important for dance as it is for tumbling or uneven parallel bar work or vaulting. Place the dance practice time at different times in the workout schedule each week. Concentration on dance technique when the gymnast is fresh at the beginning of a workout will accomplish results which will differ somewhat from those achieved at the end of a tiring workout. Each practice time has different benefits for the gymnast.

6. Use exercises to develop the strength, flexibility, and agility needed for success in dance movement. Chose exercises for explosive leg power, power in ankle extension, and development of foot strength. These exercises will also help vaulting and tumbling skills.

Beginners will find it difficult to work against their own body weight. As the gymnast improves, add weight to the body part which the gymnast must move. For example, in a routine in which the gymnast hangs from the high bar of a set of uneven bars, lifts the legs to an L hold, straddles the legs slowly, brings them back together, and lowers them slowly, add a pound weight to each foot at first and add more weight gradually. The work load must be increased for improvement. Use exercises in which the gymnast pushes against an immovable object. For example, with arms placed out in front of the body parallel to the floor and hands placed upon a table or ledge, the gymnast should try to push the table or ledge straight down into the floor. Count to ten slowly, relax for a ten count, and repeat the exercise.

Finish each workout by relating exercises to specific skills for motivation. Keep the pace rapid. Challenge the gymnasts by contests to accomplish a number of repetitions, to lift a certain weight load, or to accomplish a skill goal.

6

*Floor Exercise**

CAROLYN OSBORN BOWERS

INTRODUCTION

An excellent floor exercise routine is a complicated development of movement combinations which the gymnast integrates according to her abilities, physical structure, and temperament. When performing, the gymnast should execute her composition with rhythm, perfection of technique, and an easy gracefulness. She should be able to control her body during each second of performance and yet exercise a natural freedom within her conscious control of each movement. The excellent performance will appear correct in each movement, related to each beat of musical accompaniment, and expressing a mood of perfection.

Floor exercise is unique in that there are not the limitations of apparatus characteristic of other events. The gymnast has only the dimensions of the floor area to restrain her. The only other limitations are those of individual ability. Sometimes self-consciousness arises because of this unique feature. The gymnast must learn to consider the floor area as an apparatus to be used in its entirety. She must plan an approach to the event and to the use of the floor which will help her overcome her own weaknesses in performance. The gymnast must work hard, taking logical steps to achieve the development which will enable her to use her body freely and naturally in a well-calculated design.

*The author wishes to express her appreciation to Mr. John White, Assistant Professor of Physical Education at Bowling Green State University, for consultation concerning the skill drawings in figures 6-9 through 6-12.

GENERAL CHARACTERISTICS OF THE EVENT

The gymnast's use of the floor area, the types of movement she may select, and the qualities of control she demonstrates in these types are essential to the total impression she makes in her floor exercise routine. The following points are of prime importance.

1. Effective use of the 12x12 meter floor area is essential to the supporting structure of the routine. A floor pattern which displays versatility is constructed with the following elements in mind:
   a. Movement which travels to all parts of the floor area: near all sides, near each of the four corners, and across the middle.
   b. Placement of the difficulties at different points around the floor area.
   c. Directional changes in places other than the corners only.
   d. Curvilinear as well as straight paths.
   e. Balanced use of the floor area (not remaining in one section too long and not returning to one section repeatedly to the exclusion of the rest of the floor area).
2. The gymnast should demonstrate the following evidence of good coordination:
   a. Sureness of tumbling, acrobatics and pivots, and good balance throughout the exercise.
   b. Definition of movement, demonstrating a firm and steady body.
   c. Elegance in the stretch and carriage of the body.

d. Explosive power for tumbling, leaps, and jumps.

e. Lightness in landing from leaps and tumbling.

f. Maximum amplitude in all parts of the exercise.

g. Perfect coordination of arm and leg movements with trunk movements.

h. A supple body, despite the demand for firmness and steady execution. Correct coordination will allow for supple arms and rhythmic use of the trunk.

3. A wide selection of movements should be harmonized throughout the routine and at the same time build to a climatic finish. The choice of movements may be made from:

a. The elements of difficulty, which should include choices from tumbling, acrobatics, and dance. The four medium and two superior difficulties should be spaced throughout the routine and should be surrounded by sequences which have equal value and provide appropriate transitions.

b. Dance elements, including pivots on half-toe, leaps, jumps, and rhythmic patterns. Ballet, modern dance, jazz, and ethnic dance may be represented.

c. Tumbling and acrobatic elements which move forward, backward, and sideways.

d. Transitional movements which produce a unified gymnastic style in the combinations of tumbling, acrobatics, and dance. The beauty, rhythm, and excitement of the performance are enhanced by the manner in which the gymnast moves from one element to the next.

4. The total impression of the floor exercise routine is enhanced by the following elements:

a. The gymnast's expressiveness within each musical phrase.

b. Her ease of performance and joy in movement.

c. Her awareness of the body in space and full use of the space available.

d. Her ability to focus correctly for the most effective expression and body line.

e. Her choice and execution of beginning and ending movements and poses (for example, strong; abrupt; fading; soft, etc.).

f. Her style and coordination of movement with music.

In summation, the floor exercise routine must be lively and exciting. It must demonstrate changes in the quality and pace of movement and variety in the types of movement selected.

With the careful coordination of diverse rhythms, each sequence should add to the total impression of poetry in motion. Effective rhythms and pacing can give the routine vitality in addition to an increased technical value.

Each sequence should possess originality and an individual character which dramatizes the attributes of the gymnast. She should make the performance of her routine a presentation of herself which demonstrates confidence and style.

COMPOSITION

The manner in which a gymnast develops a floor exercise routine will differ with each individual. Certain methods can be used to initiate groups of people to the event. There are also stock routines which the beginning or intermediate gymnast can copy to learn the rudiments of moving on the floor area. Compulsory routines should be utilized to introduce gymnasts to many different styles and combinations. Beyond this stage of development, the work must be suited to the individual. The individual will utilize group drills to learn skills which may be placed in her composition, but skills which are chosen and the style with which they are assimilated should demonstrate the uniqueness of the performer.

Of the four events, the floor exercise event allows for the greatest exploration of movement. The gymnast may explore body positions with new arm and leg designs to extend her abilities. Even the best gymnasts never stop seeking new patterns for routines.

In one approach to composition, the gymnast begins by spacing her best skills equally throughout the routine. She is then faced with the selection of movement combinations which will develop her floor pattern and carry her from one major skill to the next. She must analyze where she will need relaxation prior to a very difficult sequence and where the pace may be continuous and rapid. The choice of movements used to develop the skeleton routine into a complete composition will determine the style of the performance. Such movements will also make the routine look either original or standard.

Originality involves the performer's ability to move into or out of the fullest extension of a movement in a unique way. The exploration which leads to unusual sequences showing individual style is time-consuming but may be very exciting. The coach must allow students to work on unusual combinations even if they look awkward in the beginning. With development, an awkward combination may become acceptable. Sometimes a mistake becomes the basis for an interesting movement. Regardless of the way in which new movements are found, however, they should not be used within the routine until the execution is perfected.

As the gymnast progresses she will discover her innate ability for certain types of skills. She will also discover her limitations in other movements. For example, she may have the elasticity for high tumbling and leaping and yet lack flexibility. These factors will cause her style to be different from that of the gymnast who is extremely flexible and has had, perhaps, an excellent dance background. Each of these gymnasts must choose appropriate skills from the diverse categories of movement and must also select music to suit the style of her routine.

Content of a Floor Exercise Routine

In choosing her skills for a routine, the gymnast should consider a number of factors carefully. The following example will demonstrate the development of a floor exercise composition for a gymnast who has a facility for tumbling.

Her first optional routine may include a diving cartwheel, run to a stag leap, slow cartwheel to a backward extension roll, forward handspring into a tinsica, straddle jump, and standing backward handspring. These movements should be spaced progressively throughout the routine and accompanied with appropriate music.

Variety in moving rhythmically is a singularly important factor in the routine. In the rhythmic content of a performance, one gymnast may demonstrate an element with soft music, while another may use a rapid dynamic passage. Using a variety of underlying beats will help the gymnast vary her styles of movement within a routine. An alternation between slow, soft movements and fast, explosive movements dramatizes the gymnast's ability. Control of movements in extreme tempos becomes more exciting as elements of surprise are added to a routine. The gymnast should develop the ability to change qualities of presentation. She must look strong and explosive, but she must also demonstrate softness, feminity, suppleness, and elegance.

The example routine must utilize additional skills from tumbling, acrobatics, pivots on the feet or hands, leaps, jumps, hops, balances on the feet or hands, running steps, trunk movements coordinated with locomotor movements, and selected movements from ballet, modern dance, folk dance, or (sparingly) jazz dance.

Ideally the routine will include something from each of these categories: elegant walks; running steps;

a bouncy polka pattern; a combination including an arch jump, hops, and a turning leap; pirouettes of several different styles; a swinging trunk movement with a changing arm pattern; poses such as a deep lunge and a kneeling position; and various low-level movements. As the gymnast improves she should work on distinctive alternations in tempo and quality. She should also work to add superior difficulties to her routine. It is best to include difficulties which stem from totally different combinations of movements and demonstrate differing skills. The example routine might utilize a front handspring and front somersault in place of the front handspring-tinsica combination. A second superior difficulty could be a roundoff, backward handspring, layout back somersault combination. Until the gymnast has the stamina to perform the superior movements in the latter part of her routine, she might use the layout back-somersault combination as a beginning movement in place of the diving cartwheel-stag leap sequence.

The entire routine should be executed without the mistakes and breaks of fatigue. Everything should be precise. Wise placement of fast and slow passages will help reduce fatigue and also add interest to the routine. Wise placement of the difficulties, governed by the development of the gymnast, will also produce better results.

Compositional Pointers

The gymnast should avoid:

1. Overuse of one style of dance, one type of leap, and one style of pivot.
2. Dance skills which are inapplicable to gymnastic style (lacking in transitional qualities or not adaptable in use).
3. Repetitions of a movement unless they are executed in succession. A maximum of three can be used for an increase in difficulty. For example, one could perform two aerial cartwheels in succession, or three high turning leaps which are performed with at least equal amplitude and strength.
4. Use of movement combinations from the compulsory routine (penalty assessed according to how much of the routine is like the compulsory).
5. Use of loud background music.
6. Use of connecting parts which are of less difficulty than the major elements of the routine (for example, the use of basic slides, runs, hops, and walks as connections for a routine which includes all the required difficulties).
7. Placement of all difficulties in one portion of the routine.

On the other hand, the gymnast should:

1. Develop enough stamina to distribute the difficulties throughout the routine and place one of the superior difficulties toward the conclusion.
2. Place one element of difficulty, medium or superior, in every pass.
3. Use opening and closing passages which have a technical value equal to the abilities of the gymnast as demonstrated in the rest of the routine.
4. Develop sequences which demonstrate the body type and temperament of the gymnast.
5. Use sequences which relate to the difficulties and transitions which make the movements between the difficulties gymnastically appropriate.
6. Choose music which coordinates completely with the movement, style, and physical structure of the gymnast.

The general impression of the routine is affected by the gymnast's use of music and skills, her posture and carriage throughout, her precision of execution, and her expressiveness.

There is an international interest in the use of music

which mirrors the gymnast's movement. The music must not overpower the gymnast or her performance. Instead, the routine and the music should enhance each other's effect. The FIG, for example, emphasizes that music should aid and support the gymnast. Fatigue can be reduced by changes in rhythm and speed. The timing of skills may be aided by music which prompts a more efficient expenditure of energy. Music can increase the feeling of the gymnast for her movement. It should inspire a greater depth of expression so as to increase the artistic value of the routine. Practice with the music helps develop an ease of performance and natural expression and may help to eliminate a forced smile, sticking the tongue out, and talking while performing. Coordination of music and skill aids confidence.

Both tumbling and dance may be performed with a variety of movement qualities. The force of the movement, the choice of subsequent movements, the flow of the movements, and the amount of space used can change a single skill so that it can be used in totally different presentations. Each gymnast must analyze her ability to synchronize certain types of movement with different qualities of music. Different gymnasts may use the same skill with soft or dynamic music.

Success in composition is very difficult to dissect. Every element affects another in some manner. Even the use of the concrete elements of composition is perplexing to coaches and gymnasts because of the personal nature of each routine. A good sequence may look completely wrong for some gymnasts. The structure of sequences will ultimately affect execution, amplitude, and, finally, the general expression.

SPECIFIC PENALTIES AND DEDUCTIONS FOR FLOOR EXERCISE

The specific dimensions of the floor area are 12 x 12 meters (39 feet ⅜ inches x 39 feet ⅜ inches). It is preferable that the area be covered by a thin mat which is stretched tight and anchored to the floor or is solid enough to remain firm underfoot. Common types in use in the United States are (1) canvas over a thin underpadding, (2) the composition or rubber-cured type, and (3) the thin carpet covering over padding, the latest in international competitive pads. When the bare gymnasium floor is used, a wide band of contrasting color should designate the outer boundaries of the area.

The duration of the exercise is from 1 minute to 1 minute 30 seconds.

The following timing procedures are observed:

1. The clock starts as soon as the gymnast begins a movement of the exercise. The clock will stop when the gymnast stops herself in a final pose.
2. A signal warns the gymnast at 1 minute 25 seconds.
3. A second signal sounds at 1 minute 30 seconds.

Exercises that are too short are penalized by 0.05 point for each second under 1 minute in time.

Exercises that are too long are penalized by 0.30 point. Should a gymnast continue to perform after the second signal, the judges are not obligated to judge this additional portion of performance and will evaluate the routine up to the sound of the signal. For lack of coordination between the end of the exercise and the music, a deduction of up to 0.50 point is taken from composition by each judge in addition to the technical deduction taken by the superior judge for overtime. Deductions for time penalties are taken from the average of the two middle scores by the superior judge.

It is very important that the gymnast quickly assume a definite pose or stance prior to the opening movement of her routine if she chooses to let music play before her own beginning. (It is difficult for the timers to be accurate when music is playing while the gymnast walks onto the floor; therefore, the FIG has forbidden musical accompaniment during the walk-on.) The gymnast should hold the finish pose to demonstrate the ending of the exercise. She should then return to attention and acknowledge the superior judge before walking off the floor.

Should the gymnast stop and begin the exercise again because of personal fault, the penalty will be 1.0; this penalty is deducted from the judges' total score for the exercise, when deductions for falls are made. If an incident is caused by something technical in nature (for example, an individual placing the wrong music on a tape recorder, the timer's watches not functioning, or outside interference coming within the floor area), the judges will meet with the superior judge to discuss the situation. No repetition of either compulsory or optional is allowed unless the superior judge agrees to a fault in the apparatus.

During the floor exercise event, no aid may be given to the gymnast during performance and it is forbidden for the coach to place herself on the platform. In most gymnasium situations this means along the boundaries of the floor exercise area.

Penalties specific to the performer and to actions of the coach are given in the following situations:

1. Gymnast warms up on floor area while judges are evaluating the previous performance or are in consultation: 0.50.
2. Gymnast begins exercise without presentation to the superior judge: 0.20.
3. Incorrect uniform is worn: 0.30.
4. Coach is on floor area: 0.50.
5. Signals are given from the coach to the competitor: 0.30.
6. Coach speaks to the gymnast or reverse: 0.50.
7. Beginning of the exercise is missed by personal error: 1.00.
8. Gymnast begins exercise when red light is on: no score.

The general faults are classified as small, medium, and serious errors and are related to execution and amplitude.

1. Small faults: 0.1 to 0.20 point deducted. If the small error is overshadowed by a medium or serious error, the small error is forgotten.
   a. Poor posture of the hands or head, flexion of the feet: 0.10.
   b. Slight flexion of the legs, arms, or slight straddling of the legs up to 45 degrees: 0.10.
      Examples:
      (1) Loose knees not extended tightly during leaps, walkovers, or arabesque.
      (2) Slight bend of arm during handstand or handsprings.
      (3) Legs straddling during backward handsprings, limberovers, or forward handsprings.
   c. Movements executed with a slight lack in the strength of precision, stretch, or height (amplitude): 0.20.

d. Finishing of leaps, jumps, and tumbling without lightness and suppleness or with slight lack of balance compensated by small body or arm movement: 0.20.

e. Use of a step or hop to regain balance, loss of continuity between movements, or a break in the general rhythm of the sequence: 0.20.

f. Turns not executed on the ball of the foot: 0.20.

g. Brushing the floor with the feet during a shoot-through, or split between the arms from handstands or handsprings: 0.10-0.20.

h. Somersaults under head line: 0.10-0.20.

i. Imperfect layout or degree of tuck: 0.20.

j. Legs open or flexed on back handsprings: 0.10-0.20.

k. Too much preparation before difficult acrobatics or too much running: 0.10-0.20.

l. Acrobatics out of line, or poor direction in tumbling: 0.10.

m. Too many acrobatics in a pass: 0.10.

n. Lack of continuity in what should be a quick series of dynamic acrobatic movements: 0.20.

o. Beginning a floor exercise with one of the basic ballet positions: 0.20.

p. Lack of confidence in presentation of the gymnast, especially while taking her place on the floor to begin; lack of body alignment or poor posture in opening: 0.20.

q. Faulty rhythm during the exercise (each time): 0.20.

r. Gymnast remaining too long in one place and not covering the area properly: 0.10-0.20.

2. Medium faults: 0.30 to 0.40 point deducted.

a. An obvious bending (45 degrees to 90 degrees) of the arms, legs, or body or straddling of the legs: 0.30.

b. Definite lack of amplitude: 0.30.
   Examples:
   (1) Very difficult leaps not showing height or giving the illusion of floating in the air; weak take-off.
   (2) Poor body alignment or poor extension in movements.
   (3) Failure to reach full split positions.
   (4) Somersaults under the shoulder line: 0.30 to 0.40.

c. Poor transitions, hesitations, or definite breaks in continuity (throughout the exercise): 0.30.

3. Serious faults: starting at 0.50 point deduction.

a. Extreme form breaks; bending (over 90 degrees) of the arms, legs, or body: 0.50.

b. Total lack of amplitude throughout exercise: 1.50.

    c. Repeated balance problems: 0.50.
       Example: inability to show poses with control, falling out of turning movements, poor balance out of tumbling movements, and inability to complete balance movements such as a handstand position.
    d. Slipping or losing balance to fall to floor or make necessary definite support by the hands (each time): 1.0.
    e. Fall to the floor after a difficulty: 1.0.
    f. Fall after a superior difficulty with a well executed cover up: 0.50.
    g. Overall lack of smoothness and transition, with very abrupt, stiff, and jerky execution: 0.50.
    h. Repetition of a difficulty that caused a major break or a fall: 0.50.

Neutral deductions are those deductions taken from the total score after the judge evaluates the routine. In floor exercise neutral deductions are made for:

1. Falls (each): 1.0.
2. Music not following regulations in that more than one instrument is used: 1.0.
3. Gymnast supported on a body part located outside of the floor area (for example, one or two feet completely outside of the boundary or a split position with the center of the body weight over the boundary line): 0.10 for each occurrence.
4. All penalties listed on page 69 specific to the performer and to actions of the coach.

Penalties specific to originality, general composition, combination, content and general impression of the exercise are listed below. Although some of these penalties are not listed in the official Code of Points, they are taken from notes of the International Judges' Course offered in Rome by the FIG in 1968, in the United States of America in 1970, and in Madrid in 1971. These notes have been made available by Mrs. Jackie Uphues Fie.

1. Music not adapted to the exercise (inappropriate rhythm, poor harmony of exercise and music, or poor choice of music): 0.20 to 0.50.
2. Disharmony of music and movement on ending. (The music continues after the performer has finished or stops before the performer has reached her final movement.): up to 0.50.
3. Serious discord of music and movement throughout: up to 0.50.
4. Poor distribution of difficulty throughout the exercise (for example, placing of all superiors in the first section of the exercise): 0.30.
5. Repetition of difficulties stemming from the same base with the exclusion of other difficulties (for example, several difficulties stemming from the roundoff back handspring): up to 0.50.

6. Lack of expressiveness, dynamism, ease of execution, lightness, gracefulness, elegance, and the ability to perform expressively to music: 0.10.

7. Performance of combinations of difficulties, passes, and transitions too advanced for the gymnast: up to 0.50. (A gymnast having medium and serious breaks throughout her difficulties and showing pauses and breaks in continuity before and after the more difficult movements and parts will loose additional points for choosing a composition beyond her performance level.)

COACHING HINTS TO INCREASE INDIVIDUAL SCORES
Use of the Compulsory Routine

The gymnast's first experience with complete routines should be with the use of compulsory routines. Since the competitive situation places the gymnast under a magnifying glass, the need for early exposure to compulsory routines is very important. Area coaches should plan small development meets using only compulsory routines.

Compulsory routines can help to accomplish many goals. A few of these are listed below:

1. The compulsory routine increases the gymnast's ability to remember movement patterns and to gain a feeling for direction, size, and space. In an original composition, the gymnast does not at first have such definite patterns as in a compulsory routine. The mistakes made by forgetting parts of a routine may be demonstrated more adequately when a compulsory routine is used which has definite instructions in movement design. The importance of correct arm usage should be emphasized. A gymnast must learn to think ahead in movement in order to accomplish the floor patterns. These valuable lessons will aid the first optional efforts.

2. The compulsory routine forces the gymnast to use a proportionate amount of arm movement with the body action. (Most beginners use either too much arm movement or none at all.)

3. Through compulsory routines, the gymnast begins to discover which types of movements are most suited to her, so that she can begin to develop a style.

4. The importance of learning the fundamental tumbling and dance moves and turning to either side or leading with either the left or right is discovered when the gymnast is faced by the decision to relearn one movement or reverse the entire routine.

5. The compulsory routine permits the gymnast to work in many ways:
   a. Emphasizing the rhythm of single moves.

    b. Emphasizing the rhythm of groups of movements and practicing in phrases.

    c. Emphasizing elegance in presentation.

    d. Emphasizing fluidity and perfection in transition.

6. The gymnast can learn to move with amplitude and develop a stylish presentation. Amplitude is the performance of each movement with the greatest possible degree of height, extension, strength, lightness, and suppleness. Examples to which the term "amplitude" applies are the height, strength, and extension of leaps; the execution of an arched line with the entire body; the stretching of a movement from the center of the body with such fluidity that it seems to go beyond the fingertips; and the demonstration of maximum flexibility without the loss of solid body control.

7. The gymnast can begin to condition for the endurance needed in complete routine performance.

Preparation for an Optional Routine

Workouts can provide preparation for the initial optional routine while the gymnast is preparing the compulsory for competition. The gymnast should have the fun and opportunity of trying a wide variety of skills. Coaches must have patience and encourage individual exploration in the use of the various skills. The physical stature of each girl, her abilities, and her personality are all involved in her success in learning skills and the effective use of these skills.

The gymnast must begin to plan her routine with a realistic approach. Often the first optional routine has monotonous gaps where the gymnast hopes to place a difficulty or combination which is yet to be perfected. The gymnast may compete for an entire season with an incomplete routine. To avoid this the gymnast should design movement for the *entire* routine, replacing sections only when better skills are perfected and smoothly worked into the design. (Review the general characteristics section for insight into the variety of skills from which a selection may be made. Review the composition section for an approach to composing a new routine.)

A wide variety of skills which may be performed with a degree of perfection and elegance will enhance the routine much more quickly than a group of poorly executed difficulties. Of course, the difficulties are not to be ignored and should be introduced as the gymnast progresses.

Initially the beginner or intermediate gymnast may draw upon her past movement background for ideas in transitional patterns. A bowling approach may lend a different rhythm for a locomotor pattern. A tennis backhand might be just right for a stylized pose movement. Many different sports may suggest a creative approach to total body involvement for the novice in floor exercise composition. Such an approach may also help the novice avoid copying movements and positions which are contorted or inelegant for her.

Improving the Optional Routine

Development from the first routine toward an intermediate and finally advanced level involves gradual replacement of parts of an exercise. Top gymnasts do not change an entire floor exercise even when they wish to work with a new musical arrangement. They continue to use groups of movements which have been successful for them, rearranging them according to musical expression and the placement of new difficulties. Rearrangement of sequences may improve the distribution of difficulties, effect a climax in a routine, change the pace, and provide a greater rhythmical interest. Keeping the better sequences in routines rather than beginning from scratch insures a degree of familiarity which takes time and practice to develop. A routine will advance more rapidly when wise rearrangements and replacements are made.

Practice of the Complete Routine

Increasing individual scores for an existing routine may be accomplished many different ways. Once the routine is basically complete, there are many different and beneficial ways to practice:

1. Continue work on singular movements for perfection of amplitude, balance, timing, and form.
2. Divide the routine into groupings of three or four successive movements. Perform each of these groupings several times, concentrating on the smooth transition from one move to the next. Attempt to retain the perfection of each single part without a break in the timing of the total combination. Concentrate on the degrees of difference in timing that can occur in combinations and yet allow for perfect execution of any one part.
   a. Repeat this process, but begin in the middle of one grouping and proceed to the middle of the next.
   b. Lengthen the groupings by dividing the routine into natural phrases. Where does the movement change in quality, pause for emphasis, or show decided rhythmical difference? Practice each phrase with an emphasis on rhythm. The gymnast must learn to perform each part with precision while keeping her movement continuous through each of the rhythmical phrases.
   c. Establish a style of movement which coincides with the natural rhythms of each phrase of movement and with the musical accompaniment. Use the rhythmical cues to make each combination unique.

3. Insure that the gymnast performs the complete routine several times each week.
4. Give the gymnast as much demonstration exposure as possible.
5. Analyze the combinations which consistently have breaks in rhythm and form when the gymnast is under demonstration or competition pressure. Skills must fit into the complete routine. When they do not, they are often more detrimental than advantageous. Consider the following questions:
   a. Is the sequence poor?
   b. Should the combination be relocated because of the gymnast's lack of endurance?
   c. Should a sequence be removed completely? (Perhaps the problem sequence contains a "clutch" move which needs to be practiced a great deal for confidence.)

Concentration on Endurance

Conditioning for gymnastics may take several avenues. The gymnast should have overall cardiovascular endurance to aid her in long competitive events. She must develop strength; in floor exercise she needs, particularly, explosive leg power for leaping and tumbling and general body strength for carriage and posture. Finally, the gymnast needs specific conditioning for short routines which must be perfect in execution.

Many gymnasts do not get beyond the conditioning for strength in separate skills. They do not complete their routines until the first competitive events are scheduled. In order to reach an adequate state of conditioning, the routine *must* be completed far in advance of the competitive season. Otherwise the latter parts of the routine will always be slow and without precision. The coach and gymnast will not discover where there are lags in the overall timing of movement related to music without many repetitions of full routines performed with the correct musical accompaniment.

Workouts must include the practice of full routines in each event at least once a week. This is a minimum requirement. The stage of the gymnast's development will dictate how many full routines per day or per week should be performed. The following are guidelines:
   1. When the skeleton of the routine has been assembled, the gymnast should perform to music from beginning to end exactly what is finished at each floor exercise workout. She should rest a few minutes and repeat. The rest of the workout can then be used for analysis of music and the composition of movement for the parts of the routine not yet completed.
   2. As the routine is completed, the gymnast should work with short combinations for perfection. She should also try to perform one-third or one-

half of the routine, take a rest lasting just a minute, and proceed to the next section. The entire routine should be performed in this manner at least twice.

3. The gymnast should progress to performing one full routine at each floor exercise workout. One day should be set aside to concentrate on the completed routine. On this day, the gymnast should perform, have a short rest while someone analyzes the number of faults in the performance, and then repeat the routine immediately. Working in pairs, the entire team may follow this process, each girl performing four complete routines in about a half an hour, with a slightly longer rest between the first two and the second two repetitions. A final evaluation should be made to determine specific parts of the routine which will need practice another day.

A Potpourri of Ideas

Wall posters may be used as an incentive toward perfect full routines. Improvement in the number of breaks may be recorded or a club may be established for girls who perform a number of good routines successively with a short rest between.

The placement of difficulties should be planned according to the gymnast's current endurance ability. When a difficulty is newly perfected and the gymnast is less experienced, perhaps the difficulty should be placed toward the beginning of the routine. When the gymnast is capable of performing the difficult combination in a more appropriate position without apparent fatigue, she may shift it. For example, an entire tumbling pass may replace movements used temporarily. Every practice should conclude with exercises for endurance and the development of strength. The exercises may range from those providing general conditioning to those providing specific muscle development.

Practices immediately prior to a competitive event should be very light workouts. The gymnast should stretch thoroughly and work on troublesome parts of the routine just a few times. The total routine should be performed once with maximum effort. The gymnast should walk through her floor pattern several times, using arm designs, assuming poses, and perhaps executing the easy tumbling moves. While she does this she should mentally review the rhythms of all combinations. She may then help to set her rhythmic pace just before the competitive performance by this type of mental review and walkthrough on the sidelines.

A change in a routine should not be made just prior to a competitive event, unless it involves the deletion of a single move which is particularly troublesome. A replacement combination should receive a concentrated bit of attention so that it will not be forgotten or cause a major break in rhythm.

Each season should be planned for competitions, for times to rework routines, and for times to change music. Major routine changes and new music should not be attempted until the end of the competitive schedule in preparation for another year.

A new combination of moves or a new difficulty should not be used simply because the gymnast has performed it correctly a few times. A rule of thumb is to insure that the movement is performed well in at least eight out of ten tries over a span of at least ten workouts before even considering its use in the competitive situation. At first the movement should be used in demonstration situations if at all possible.

The gymnast and coach should be realistic in planning ahead for the relocation of moves of difficulty. The gymnast should not go through an entire season planning to use a movement in a particular place if such a movement is very difficult to perfect.

Music

When selecting or changing music, follow these steps:

1. Choose a melody which the gymnast likes and which wears well.
2. Try to determine the gymnast's most natural style: large and slow, large and rapid, bouncy and quick, or smooth and melodic.
3. Find music predominantly suited to the style of the gymnast.
4. When combining several selections, ensure that the music has correct transitions and that the changes are not too abrupt. A medley which does not have musically correct changes between melodies and rhythms will create problems in flow even before the composition has been created.
5. Use accents to help spark the routine.
6. Make sure that there are musical phrases which will force the gymnast to vary her style and speed of movement.

If pre-recorded music (not specifically arranged to fit the routine) is used, follow these steps:

1. Place the difficulties within the routine structure with regard for the gymnast's stamina and the appropriateness of the music.
2. Use combinations of movements which will be retained within the new musical framework. They may be moved from the beginning to the end or from the middle to the first pass. Placement will depend upon the music. New movements to fit several beats or even just two counts may have to be added between combinations retained from the previous routine.
3. Spend some time planning the effect of the beginning of the routine and the finishing combinations. For example, if a gymnast lacks the ability for high leaps, perhaps her finish pose should be a high stretching movement. If the gymnast has such ability, she may wish to move rapidly to

a low-level pose. Do not plan an abrupt tumbling-to-pose ending if the gymnast lacks stamina. It is certain to leave with the judges an impression of unsteadiness and weakness.

Effective Use of Space

The gymnast, like the dancer, must train her body as a strong instrument to be used for movement in space. The gymnast performs alone and has no single stage side for an audience. Her problem is unique in that her composition must be alive and pulsating in a space which faces in all directions.

The development of awareness of the body in space and the effective use of space by a gymnast takes time and practice. The gymnast must learn to feel where her body parts are, to know how long it takes them to arrive in a particular position, and even to feel exactly where they should stop. She must learn to feel amplitude at the same time she disciplines herself not to go beyond a definite point in body placement. Rhythm within a movement will combine time, pace, and meter. In effect, these must all be "placed in space" by the strength and physical stature of the gymnast.

A few fortunate individuals have a natural flair for presentation. They move in space quite easily. Most gymnasts have to work very hard to learn the most effective head placement, focus, and limb placement for maintenance of an aesthetic line.

The timing of coordinated arm and leg movements is often wrong because the gymnast is not aware of how far the arms and legs must travel and where the movement should stop. Movements must be deliberately planned. The gymnast must be able to repeat them exactly so as to create unfailingly the visual impression of parts related to a whole.

The following are suggestions for the development of a kinesthetic feeling for the body in space:

1. Movement exercises may be used which combine a given rhythm for locomotion and a coordinated arm movement. For example, walk four steps, moving the arms from the sides to positions in which one arm is vertical and the other forward horizontal. One arm will have to move twice as fast to reach the vertical at the same time in which the other reaches the forward horizontal and the last step is completed. Patterns like this may be simple or complex. They may involve turns, uneven strides, various locomotor skills, the movement of arms together or separately, and coordinated torso movement. The exercises may be both challenging and fun at the end of a workout.

2. Compulsory ·routines can be visually analyzed and compared with good performances by the use of films or video tapes. Shortening of the body line, covering the face by a poor arm position, strained lifting of the

shoulders, and many other faults which affect body line and elegance can be pointed out.

3. Another person may actually stop the arms in motion in a correct position or may physically straighten or turn a leg. Much like spotting for learning purposes, it often is beneficial to help the gymnast through a movement correctly. The feel of the movement thus begins to be part of a motor pattern.

4. Mirrors should be used for practice of body line and position as follows:
    a. With her back to the mirror the gymnast may assume the position as she "feels" it is correct. She may then turn to face the mirror and be corrected to the proper position.
    b. She may move through a sequence while watching the arms and legs function together.

5. The coach may ask the gymnast to perform sequences with movements as large as possible. Generally the gymnast will be out of control, but the exercise will give her a different sense of proportion in space and movement. Parts of the routine which should be large may be practiced for control. The gymnast may become better able to experience freedom of movement and also the excitement of contrast by using this device.

6. Gymnasts should view good technique and learn critical points related to the management of space and rhythm. They should learn judging and know what the judges are looking for. They may then work in pairs or small groups to discuss point deductions in each other's performances.

TECHNICAL ANALYSIS OF SELECTED FLOOR EXERCISE MOVEMENTS

Analysis of tumbling and dance movements will be made within the separate chapters dealing with these subjects. In addition to tumbling and dance, there are movements which are often used specifically in floor exercise. These are unique in their manner of combination, are more acrobatic in nature, or have evolved through creative efforts within the event. The following selected movements are analyzed and errors in performance are described.

Movements Demonstrating Flexibility and Suppleness

Good Technique	Common Technical Errors	Results
Body Wave		
May be executed from a squat, half-squat, or slight flexion of the body. It is a forward pushing	Over-arch in the lower back (abdomen not held in control, or lack of arch in upper back).	Jerky execution; the movement is stiff. A lack of rhythm and suppleness.

Good Technique	Common Technical Errors	Results
movement begun in the knees and going to the hips, abdomen, chest and finally the head. One or both arms may sweep backward as the wave begins, to be circled rearward and upward, with the arch ending overhead in the stretched standing position. It must be fluid and supple.	Arms not coordinated with body movement.	Timing is poor; exercise appears as segmented movements rather than as a designed flow.

Step Kick

Good Technique	Common Technical Errors	Results
May be executed to the side or front. Both legs should be turned out for maximum stretch. The kick should move quickly to the vertical; the supporting leg must be straight. Sometimes the kicking leg is caught and held in a balanced pose. It should be caught above 90 degrees, not caught part way up and pulled into position.	Kick too low to demonstrate amplitude.	Heavy or stiff. Fault in flexibility of body demonstrated.
	Knees not extended.	Poor form deduction for bent legs. Awkwardness.
	Catching leg to pull up.	Lack of muscular control for leg lift. Slowness, without excitement.

Side Split

Good Technique	Common Technical Errors	Results
Both legs must be stretched directly to the side; the split should be flat unless it is very low and still shows support as a straddle stand, with hips backward and body inclined forward. Movements into and out of this movement must be carefully designed so as not to be awkward. The split does not have to be held.	Awkward transitions into or out of flexibility position.	Buttocks dominant. Lack of elegance. Lack of continuity.
	Split incomplete.	Insufficient amplitude. Poor design and combination.

Good Technique	Common Technical Errors	Results

Rolling Through a Straddle

Generally executed from a movement with some forward momentum, such as a forward roll or headspring to straddle sit. The feet grip the floor as the body lifts. The hips are extended, and there is a slight arch in the torso in order to roll forward onto the abdomen. The movement must be smooth and low enough to demonstrate flexibility.

Hips are not extended for a smooth roll; gymnast falls forward in a slight pike.

Lack of rhythm.
Execution not smooth.
Heaviness.
If pike is extreme, it appears as a mistake.

Arm Support Movements

Handstand Switch Kick

The gymnast kicks toward the handstand position but allows the lead leg to split overhead. The shoulders and back must still be extended. A complete split is reached and the legs are switched through a straight handstand to return to a split. The hips are stretched upward, the abdomen tightened inward, and the lead leg lowered to the floor. The legs remain split as long as possible until movement into the following combination.

Lead leg is not far enough over to show initial split.

Movement does not continue smoothly from beginning to end.

Lack of extension in shoulders and back.

Insufficient amplitude.
Lack of rhythm.

Break in rhythm.
Unnecessary stop in handstand.
Jerkiness.
Lack of elegance.

Loss of balance.
Sagging appearance.
Strain in body

Balanced Press Movements

The arms must be straight; a woman must not demonstrate a muscular "push-up" press. Counter-

Gymnast jumps into the movement.

Not a true press.

Good Technique	Common Technical Errors	Results

balance at the shoulders. The hips are directly above the support with the shoulders leaning forward as the leg lift or lowering begins. The movement should be continuous and appear to be easy.

Counterbalance of the shoulders is not quite enough; legs, moving slowly, come to a stop in the middle of the execution.

Lack of rhythm.
Lack of continuity.
Strain.
Rush at finish.

Backward Walkover to Splits

The gymnast should move off of one foot to the hands. She must extend very hard in the shoulders. The legs are split. The back is flattened as the lead leg is pulled toward the chest and between the arms. The gymnast should lower her body directly into the split position.

Walkover does not extend upward in a good vertical support.
Extra extension and back not flattened just as foot is to pass between arms.

Shoulders do not have a slight forward lean for counterbalance.

Brush or catch of lead foot on floor.
Lead foot touches to split behind hands.
Lack of rhythm.
Lack of continuity.

Split occurs behind hand position.
Finish is too sudden.
Heaviness.

6.1   Press Handstand

A.   Place hands close to feet. Hips will move forward over base of support.

B.   Forward lean of shoulders counterbalances as legs are raised. Hips over hand support.

C.   Body in balance over base of support. Lift by back as well as legs.

D.   Shoulders move back as hips and legs move up toward good handstand position. (See also the chapter on tumbling.)

Good Technique | *Common Technical Errors* | *Results*

Backward Handspring to Splits

(For backward handspring execution see chapter on tumbling.)
The execution position into the split is much like that for the walkover to splits. The exception is the two-foot spring: the legs will separate at the vertical position, one pulling sharply to the chest to pass between the legs. The movement between arch and extension of the back is more rapid than for the walkover. The throw for the handspring is softer than in a series of tumbling handsprings.

Same faults as listed for backward walkover to splits.

Handspring too rapid or not extended enough with a good push from the legs.

Same results as listed for backward walkover to splits.

Heaviness.
Bend in forward leg to pass between arms.

6.2   Valdez

A.   Starting position. Arms may be reversed.

B.   Bent leg begins to push, chest lifts, arm reaches upward and backward, and head looks back.

C.   Bent leg continues to push; straight leg lifts. Body arches as arm continues to reach up and over.

D.   Force carries hips upward over base of support. A true Valdez is executed into a good handstand position. Floor exercise variations may show a split handstand or walkover into another element.

Valdez

Executed from a sitting position with one leg extended and the other leg bent with the foot placed close to the hips. Either arm may be placed back on the floor, palm

Looking sideways over the support arm and shoulder.
Throwing arm across body rather than straight up and rearward.

Gymnast twists to cartwheel.
Not true valdez; no reaching or passing through handstand support. No credit.

Good Technique	Common Technical Errors	Results
flat, fingers pointing away from the hips. The other arm is extended to throw upward and back. The bent leg pushes against the floor, forcefully extending. The straight arm and leg lift up and reach backward. The body arches. The body should arrive at or pass through a good extended handstand.	Rotation of rear arm and overarch of upper body into backbend before thrust of legs.	Poor timing. Jerky and heavy.

Miscellaneous

Back Spin with Split Leg Circles

The momentum for the spin comes primarily from the forceful leg thrust. As the gymnast rolls onto her back, one leg is forcefully circled low and across the other leg and body. The second leg follows when the first leg is almost split. The gymnast spins on her upper back. The leg movement should be continuous and demonstrate flexibility.	Body does not roll smoothly onto back.	Heaviness.
	Leg motion slow and not smooth. Poorly coordinated parts.	Lack of continuity. Lack of elegance.
	Legs not low enough in relation to body.	Insufficient amplitude.
	Legs bend.	Poor form. Poor transition.

Illusion

This is a spin on one leg while the free leg and upper body rotate windmill fashion in a vertical plane. The movement should be continuous and show a split position. The leg and torso will counterbalance each other while the support leg rotates a full turn. The	Upper body lowers to leg without the leg raising to a split simultaneously.	Buttocks obvious. Poor body line. Awkwardness. Jerkiness.
	Legs do not reach split.	Awkwardness. No illusion of split rotation. No credit.

Good Technique	Common Technical Errors	Results
ending should be balanced, coming to a stand.	Working leg not held high long enough.	Rotation not complete. Lack of balance. Jerkiness. Lack of continuity.

6.3   Illusion

A. Torso is lowered while leg rises. Arched body line is maintained.
B. Support leg begins to turn; upper body brushes past on open hip side; legs reach split.
C. Leg remains high while turn is completed and upper body rises.

Tour en l'Air to Splits

The turn in the air must be in perfect balance to allow the split drop to be in balance. The gymnast pushes off legs into the air. The posture is in line and abdomen pulled in. The arms and head rotate the body. The arms extend to act as a checking agent for the spin as the feet press against the floor. The body drops rapidly but leg pressure keeps the split landing from being heavy.	Body leans too far forward.	Off balance. Stop between turn and split.
	Arms do not check spin. Body continues to rotate.	Crooked split. Off balance.
	Feet do not press against floor.	Heavy landing in split position. Body may bounce.

Good Technique   *Common Technical Errors*   *Results*

6.4 Cradle

A. Body moves off balance backward, legs and arms begin to throw, and chest lifts (less force than regular handspring).

B. Legs and hips have extended; head looks back at floor.

C. Hands touch floor; arms take support; lower body as head tucks and legs pike.

D. Shoulders are lowered to floor. Legs extend over shoulders and head to balance weight.

E. Immediate beat is applied to thrust up and out by straight legs. Arms extend and head drops back.

F. Hips are high, legs straight, and body arched. Torso helps pull upward.

Cradle (Back Handspring to Neckspring)

(For backward handspring execution, see chapter on tumbling.) The back handspring is executed more softly. When the hands reach the floor, the head is tucked, the shoulders are lowered, and the body is piked. The bounce from the tight pike should be utilized immediately to thrust the legs up and out; the hips extend and the body arches to walkout or kip to arch stand. There is no stop between closing and opening; the movement should flow smoothly. In a walkout, the legs should split. The free leg is held up in the air as for a well executed walkover. (See tumbling chapter.)

Handspring too fast.
Body collapses in pike.

Hips fall to floor.
Legs not extended upward from hips.

Free leg not held up in walkout.
Legs bend on landing (either arch stand or walkout).

Heavy landing on shoulders.
Lack of rhythm.
Lack of continuity.
Poor timing; faulty application of force.

Center of gravity too low.
Insufficient amplitude in walkout.
Loss of power; incomplete movement.

Poor technique.
Overarch in lower back.
Squat landing; hips pike.
Fall is off balance.

Good Technique	Common Technical Errors	Results

Headspring to Straddle Sit or Straight Sit

Hands are placed flat on the floor. Head is placed slightly ahead of hands with the weight just above the hairline on the forehead. The legs push the body to pass through a piked headstand position and into an overbalance. The legs thrust forward-upward and the arms push. The body extends at the hips, toes reach for the floor, and the body immediately pikes again to allow for the sitting position.

No extension of hips.

Insufficient arm push.
Poor thrust from legs.

Hips touch before feet; gymnast bounces.

Jerkiness.
Gymnast may not reach sitting position.

FLOOR EXERCISE DIFFICULTIES
Medium Difficulties

1. Leaps, jumps, and turning movements
   a. Any combination of two or three leaps in series with amplitude. The second and third leap in the series must not show less strength (or height for the particular type of leap) than the preceding leap or leaps.
   b. Leap with change of legs or scissors movement.
   c. Leap with forward leg bent in stag position. (See chapter on dance.)
   d. Leaps and jumps with half-turn.
   e. Jump bringing legs upward to demonstrate a pike body position.
   f. Jumps which arch:
      (1) Legs stretched and rearward in the line of the arch.
      (2) One leg bent rearward and the other leg extended.
      (3) Both feet reaching rearward to neck height.
   g. Turning jumps which land in a controlled balance.
   h. Well designed body and arm movement in use with a locomotor series including such movements as hops, turns, and jumps.
   i. 360-degree (or greater) turns on half-toe.
   j. Pirouette to a split or controlled balance pose.
2. Rolls
   a. Layout dive into forward roll.
   b. Use of forward roll without hands as a connecting movement and into a balanced pose.

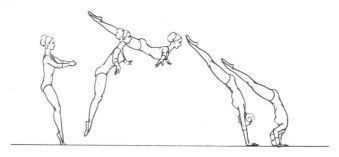

6.5   Layout Dive Roll

A. Hurdle into take-off. Feet drive forward of body in blocking action, chest lifts, and motion is upward.

B. Very slight pike on take-off as chest and hips lift.

C. Shoulders level off. Rotation point moves toward shoulders. Hips continue to rise. Body straightens into layout and begins descent.

D. Head looks to floor and tucks as hands reach floor. Legs start pike.

E. Hips move over head and shoulders. which take support. Arms still work against body weight. Legs stay back to keep tuck and balance the roll.

6.6   Backward Roll to Handstand, Split

A. Roll backward into pike.

B. Legs extend upward from hip. Arms begin to push as legs lift weight upward (head also pushes off from floor).

C. Hips are still slightly behind support as body comes close to full extension. Upward push continues until extended at shoulders, focus in front of hands. Hips slightly in front of support. Motion stopped to show control.

D. Forward leg pulls forcefully downward from the hip, moves straight toward chest. Head tucks to look at legs. Extension in shoulders.

E. Back rounds. Slight forward lean in shoulders. Feet touch simultaneously to slide on down.

F. Weight is maintained solidly on hands until full split with hips between hand support.

    c. Handstand with forward roll into immediate leap or jump.

    d. Backward roll to handstand:

        (1) Into split between the hands.

        (2) Into 180-degree pirouette on the hands and forward rollout.

        (3) Into forward walkover.

    e. Backward roll to kip to the feet, landing with an arched body.

3. Forward walkover combinations

    a. To a bridge.

        (1) Second leg extended or bent.

        (2) Touching one leg to immediate walkover.

    b. To a split.

    c. With one arm supporting.

    d. Onto two legs into a leap or jump.

    e. Into an immediate arabesque pencheé on the landing leg. (See chapter on dance.)

    f. To swing free leg backward into forward roll without hand support.

4. Backward walkover combinations

    a. With an exchange of legs while inverted.

    b. Wtih stag leg position extending to split position while inverted.

    c. To a straddle seat or straddle held off the floor in a pike position.

    d. To bring both legs together and stoop through.

5. Valdez

6. Backward tinsica (Support on one arm at a time; hand placement may not be parallel.)

6.7 Backward Tinsica

    A. May begin looking slightly over shoulder, with body twisted. Left leg will lift; upper back arches. Step off right leg and push.

    B. Sequence is hand, hand, foot, foot, with even placement and rhythm.

    C. Hand placement is separated; one arm supports at a time. Body moves into walkover type of body position.

a. As a single movement.
b. In combination.
   (1) To a split.
   (2) In a series.

6.8   Forward Tinsica

A.   From hurdle step, arms and body stretch forward and reach toward mat. Strong leg lift and push. Arms reach mat one at a time, one in front of the other.

B.   Hurdle step. Sequence of placement is hand, hand, foot, foot, with even rhythm.

C.   Legs are split. As first hand pushes off floor, first foot reaches toward floor.

D.   Second arm pushes, body lifts, and second leg acts as lever to counterbalance. Body is arched.

7. Forward tinsica
   a. In series executed in place.
   b. From a dive.
      (1) With hesitation in arm placement.
   c. From a handspring, dive.
   d. From a roundoff, half turn into dive tinsica.
8. Cartwheels
   a. Cartwheels in series using the right arm first, than the left arm, and then two arms.
   b. One-arm cartwheel which rotates; usually performed on the second arm, begun facing line of direction and rotating one-fourth turn to cartwheel position and one-fourth turn to step out facing the start.
9. Handsprings
   a. Forward handspring using only one arm.

(1) With exchange of legs while inverted.

(2) Into immediate forward handspring, supporting with other arm.

b. Forward handspring with exchange of legs.

c. Forward handspring with a walkout into immediate forward handspring, landing on two legs.

d. Forward handspring to a split.

(1) With half-turn into a split.

e. From a dive.

f. Jump to the hands, snap down with pike or bent knees and continue into a backward handspring.

g. Spring off the hands with half-turn, snapping the legs down together (roundoff).

Superior Difficulties

1. All somersaults and combinations leading into or out of somersaults*

a. Layout, piked, or tuck positions.

b. Sideways, forward, or backward direction.

c. With twists added during execution.

6.9 Front Somersault

A. Block and lift for upward direction. Powerful leg and ankle extension.

B. Hips continue to rise. Arms and head throw for rotation.

C. Body is rotating and will start downward as spin continues.

D. Body begins to open for landing (approximately three-fourths of the way around, depending upon the desired balance for next movement or pose).

E. Arms move outward to help slow rotation. Toes reach toward floor slightly in front of body as motion will bring body into balance over support.

*A somersault is a completely aerial movement, as opposed to a roll, which is executed on the ground.

6.10   Front Handspring, Front Somersault (Piked Position)

A. Feet reach out for floor, under-rotating the handspring (creates a blocking effect to help height for somie).

B. Body lifts with seat drawing hips back. Center of rotation moves toward chest.

C. Upward lift has established forces; head tucks and arms reach as body pikes into rotation.

D. Pike opens for landing. Arms reach sideward.

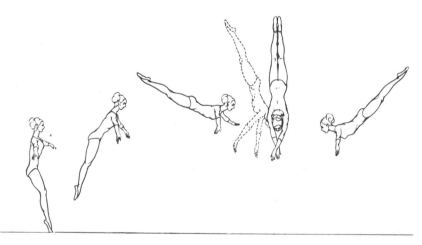

6.11   Layout Front Somersault with Half-Twist

A. From hurdle, legs swing forward and drive into floor.

B. Strong upward lift of chest and arms as forward motion is converted to upward motion. Slight pike on take-off as body lifts.

C. Hips continue to rise; rotation moves around chest and shoulders.

D. Twist begins, both arms and head effecting twist.

E. Body is descending. Arms are thrown out to stop twisting action. Strong head lift and hip thrust forward maintain layout until landing.

6.12   Roundoff, Layout Back Somersault, Full Twist

A. Hurdle step, stretch torso, strong throw of arms forward, reaching out. Hands hit mat in straight line, one at a time.

B. Legs come together overhead, body executes a half-twist, and both arms push as legs snap down and back lifts. Legs reach backward to create blocking action for upward lift of layout.

C. Chest and arms lift upward for height; head is erect. Legs and ankles have extended for strong upward drive.

D. Body begins to arch. Hip lift comes up as response to initial effort. Start rotation dropping left arm and reaching with right; then head follows immediately to help twist.

E. Left arm is passive, wrapped out of the way. Right arm rotates body but stretches (does not fall across chest) and sustains force and direction of twist.

F. Into last half of twist, all forces are accomplished. Body flight begins descent. Arm whips to come around across chest.

G. Arms check spin by reaching out, movement opens up, and hips thrust forward to keep arch.

2. Aerial walkover, aerial cartwheel, and aerial tinsica
   a. Series of aerial movements.
   b. All combinations of tumbling leading into and out of aerial movements.
3. Backward handspring combinations
   a. Cradle. (For execution of backward handspring to neckspring into an arched stand, see analysis of selected floor exercise movements.)
   b. In a series.
      (1) Series landing only on one leg each time.
   c. To a controlled handstand.
4. Leaps, jumps, or turns which rotate more than 360 degrees and finish in a balance, an immediate walkover, or another immediate movement

7

Balance Beam

JACQUELYN UPHUES FIE

INTRODUCTION

A gymnast exercising on the balance beam should strive to achieve an original combination of movements performed with such confidence, sureness, poise, and elegance that balance beam work appears to be "elevated floor exercise." The exercise must be presented in a manner that makes one forget the restricted medium upon which performance takes place.

The entire exercise must exemplify a flow of varied rhythmical movement, even though musical accompaniment is absent. The tumbling and acrobatics, dance elements, basic movement combinations, and momentary pauses must show originality in combination and design and must relate to the body structure, expressive quality, and physical abilities of the performer.

Balance and controlled movement throughout are the principal performance goals. Only those elements which can be executed with maximum control and equilibrium and yet can demonstrate freedom and ease of execution should be selected and integrated into the composition.

GENERAL CHARACTERISTICS OF BEAM EXERCISE

The general composition of a beam exercise must contain these essential elements:

1. Movements necessitating balance executed in both the upright and inverted positions, including momentary pauses with body erect, inclined forward or backward, or inverted with the weight supported on the hands.

2. Turns on the half-toe in left and right directions, with varying degrees of difficulty beyond 180 degrees.

3. Jumps and leaps showing vertical and horizontal amplitude.

4. Large and small running steps of an elongated and rhythmical nature.

5. Stepping movements with a variety of arm and leg configurations.

6. Specific dance elements drawn from ballet, modern dance, jazz, and character studies and specific combinations of a purely gymnastic nature.

7. Elements of difficulty (two of superior quality and four in the medium range) very thoughtfully and evenly placed within the composition.

8. A mount and dismount corresponding in difficulty to the internal value of the exercise.

9. Use of the total beam dimension and varied placement of the difficulties from one end to the other.

10. Good and beautiful connections on par with the difficulty of the exercise performed.

11. A reasonable number of sitting, lying, or crouched positions. (These, however, should not equal or exceed the number of upright

and stretched movements, which are by their nature both more difficult and more spectacular.)

12. No more than three stops. (A stop is a period of repose with or without the arms moving.)

The FIG Code has placed considerable emphasis on the new concept of continuous beam movement. It is now forbidden to stop all movements of the feet and simply use the arms and hands. The previous practice of hiding stops in this manner is no longer permissible. The ideal routine has continuous execution, with no pauses for stability prior to difficult passages or elements. The pace on the whole must be brisk but show an interesting variety in rhythm.

Other than technique, rhythm is the most important factor in execution. Performing an exercise slowly with stops before each element of difficulty makes the execution easier, and also reduces the value of the exercise. An exercise without rhythmical variety is correspondingly less vibrant and spectacular and possesses less vitality, even if it contains sufficient difficulty and

"V" Sit   Tight "V" Sit   Back Lever

Needle Scale   Stag Handshake   Deep Arch Lunge

7.1 Poses

demonstrates good technique. Therefore, a difficult exercise exhibiting the same rhythm throughout does not have the same technical value as the same exercise executed with changes in rhythm and animation.

The current trend in difficulty is toward execution of acrobatic elements in a series. Actual tumbling has become more dominant.

The finished exercise must include movements that demonstrate the gymnast's overall body flexibility, hidden strength, and total body coordination. The gymnast must perform this exercise with a sureness of execution showing the fullest amplitude within her range of ability. An air of confidence and a feeling of personal enjoyment should be transmitted to the audience. All of the movements should be purely feminine and carried out in an elegant manner.

TECHNICAL ANALYSIS OF SELECTED BEAM MOVEMENTS

The movements analyzed in this chapter have been selected with these criteria in mind:

1. The frequency with which they are performed.
2. The need to provide a representative sample of various types of movements: mounts, dismounts, rolls, flexibilities, wheels, handstands, turns and pivots, leaps and jumps.
3. The need to provide a balanced choice of medium and superior difficulties.
4. The importance of analyzing movements specifically used in balance beam competition.

A technical analysis of dance movements, tumbling skills, and selected floor exercise movements has been made in previous chapters. Most of these movements and combinations are applicable to the balance beam and will therefore not be repeated in this chapter. Reference to specific chapters for further detailed descriptions is made periodically.

The treatment of each skill begins with a description of good technique as viewed by the judge. The description is not intended as full instruction for the gymnast. Each description includes specific hints on how to spot good technical execution, with emphasis on amplitude or the ultimate in performance. A list of common technical errors and their effect on performance follows each description.

Mounts

Good Technique	Common Technical Errors	Results
Squat Press Mount		
Jump; place hands on beam; lift hips high; lean shoulders forward, keeping arms straight; tuck knees tightly to chest, "placing" balls of feet softly between the hands on beam, keeping head up.	Hips too low; insufficient forward lean.	Underbalance, noticeable grasping of beam, shifting of feet in squat, separation of knees.
	Poor posture and body stretch in handstand.	Excess sag or overarch in handstand; poor amplitude.
For a "press" handstand, the hands are not farther than shoulder distance apart, the shoulders lean well in front of the hands, the feet	Insufficient lean forward at shoulders, then hips. Poor degree of tuck during "press."	No continuity between mount and "press" during transfer of weight from feet to hands.

Good Technique	Common Technical Errors	Results
leave the beam without impetus, the hips move slowly over the shoulders, and the shoulders re-align over the hands when the handstand is stretched, showing no accentuation of arch or pike.		Jerky rise to handstand with small stops to catch balance. Visible show of strength in "press."

Knee Scale Mount

Good Technique	Common Technical Errors	Results
Approach may be (1) straight onto knee scale facing out, (2) straight onto jump with one-fourth turn to knee scale, or (3) oblique to knee scale. Jump to kneeling position on knee, keeping arms straight and head up and simultaneously lifting the free leg high. There will be more forward lean on method (1). When combining with the turn, begin the turn as soon as the knee scale position is fully reached. Maintain the position throughout the turn, with backward leg extended upward above 45°.	Dropping of free leg below 45°. Late raising of free leg. Leg should reach maximum elevation as opposite knee touches beam. Bending arms. Poor body angle (less than 90°) between arms and trunk and flexed thigh.	Poor continuity. Lack of balance. Insufficient amplitude.

Wolf Mount (One or one and one-half turn)

Good Technique	Common Technical Errors	Results
Same as for squat, except one leg squats between both hands and the other extends horizontally sideward. The free leg must be horizontally sideward as the squat leg contacts the beam. Shift body weight slightly sideward away from free leg and complete turn.	Body bent forward on turn. Squat leg support not on ball of foot.	Poor continuity; lengthy pause before turn; poor balance.
	Leg dropping below horizontal. Squatting prematurely. Head bowed.	Insufficient amplitude of leg and body position.

Good Technique	*Common Technical Errors*	*Results*

Straddle Mount (at side of beam)

There is a two-foot take-off, a high hip lift with lean of shoulders forward, straddle of legs 90° or more, and a placement of balls of the feet on the beam with control.	Insufficient forward lean. Bent arms, bowed head.	Underbalance; struggle to stay on beam.

Straddle Mount to Straddle "L" Hold (at side)

Hold wide straddle, legs horizontal, hips lifted well above beam.	Narrow straddle, dropping legs below horizontal.	Insufficient amplitude.

7.2   Straddle "L" Hold Press Handstand Mount

"Press" to Handstand from Straddle Stand or Straddle Hold (at end or side of beam)

The shoulders lean well in front of the hands, the hips are moved over the shoulders as the legs rise, the shoulders realign over the hands when the legs are brought together in a stretched handstand.	Insufficient lean of hips. Center of gravity still inside body. Poor stretch in handstand.	No continuity. Jerky press. Labored movement. Lack of amplitude in body stretch.

Straddle Mount to Side Split

Lower to flat split or very low straddle support with forward body lean.	Lack of full degree of split. Poor coordination and use of arms.	Insufficient amplitude. Ungraceful.

Good Technique	*Common Technical Errors*	*Results*

Straddle Mount to Rear Support

Straddle vault, clearing beam, and catch body weight on hands as legs close and extend into rear support.

Insufficient height on clearing beam.
Straddle not wide enough; piking of body throughout.

Heavy landing on beam in sitting position.

The hands touch the beam twice: once during the vault, and again for support after the legs have passed over.

Bent arms on regrasp.

Hips slide below beam during regrasp.

Scissors Mount (hitchkick to side seat half-turn free)

The hand support during the scissors to a riding seat is acceptable on a lower level. For medium difficulty, execute the scissors with a high exchange of straight legs, using no hand support, and on body contact with the beam immediately half-turn free to a riding seat.

Scissors kick too high.

Heavy landing on beam on hips or overshooting of beam.

Pause before half-turn.

Poor continuity.

Bent legs.

Poor form; no elegance.

7.3   **Forward Roll Mount**

Forward Roll Mount

The hands grasp the beam after take-off. The hips lift high before head is tucked; then the tuck and placement of the back of the neck on the beam occur. The roll is continuous, maintaining a pike, with

Poor hip elevation.

Heavy or noisy head placement instead of back of neck.

Bent arms on hip lift.

Lack of continuous movement.

Loss of pike position while rolling forward.

Obvious regrasp under beam for balance.

Good Technique	Common Technical Errors	Results

or without shifting the hands underneath the beam. The rise is immediate, progressing to the next movement.

Tucking head too soon.

Landing hard on beam with entire back. No further rotational movement possible.

7.4   Whip Forward Roll Mount

Swing Forward Roll Mount

From straddle "L" hold, the legs cast backwards, and the body is momentarily stretched. There are a quick pike and hip lift, head tuck, and forward roll.

Hand placement not close to crotch.

Weak cast backward; slow execution.

Early head tuck, hitting top of head on beam.

Inability to lean shoulders forward, move weight center over support, and lift hips sufficiently before roll.

Insufficient amplitude.

Jerky roll; heavy execution. Incomplete roll; fall.

Shoulder Stand Mount

From a two-foot takeoff with the left hand on top of the beam and the right hand underneath the beam for control (both hands on top is permissible), lift hips forcefully upward over hand support. Head is kept upward. Inverted position is reached with legs together or in full split as shown. Body makes quarter turn to left as right leg is placed on beam with knee bent next to right hand.

Too much hip lean, over-arch, or lack of control with right hand.

Failure to fully split before quarter turn.

Overbalance or show of strength to maintain inverted position.

Lack of continuity into turn and next element. Too lengthy a pause.

Good Technique   *Common Technical Errors*   *Results*

7.5   Shoulder Stand Mount

Oblique Step-on Mount

Whether executed obliquely or at the end of the beam, generally all step-on mounts must be preceded by a strong take-off and show good extension of the first kicking leg, followed by a bending of the knee in order to place the first foot on the beam. The body must be inclined slightly forward to aid the continuous momentum but must straighten out after the foot or feet are on the beam.

Poor kick and lack of extension of kicking leg.

Landing on flat foot with heel on beam instead of on ball of foot.

Low leap onto beam.
Hand support or touch to maintain balance.

Excessive body lean forward to correct balance.

7.6   Oblique Step-on Mount

Good Technique	*Common Technical Errors*	*Results*

7.7   Thief Vault Mount

Thief Mount

Look for the board placed further back to allow for a one-foot take-off and passing of the straight leg, followed by a bent leg (knee toward chest). The hands catch the weight, with legs brought together in the extended forward position, and the body straightens into a rear support.

Bending lead leg as it passes over beam.

Failure to bring legs together quickly.

Poor timing of regrasp; late catch.

Body pike, sitting on beam; show of force to correct underbalance or overbalance.

Catch foot resulting in fall.

Poor form, awkward.

Heavy hand contact, bent arms.

Unattractive; lacks fluency and aesthetic value.

7.8   Forward Walkover Mount

Spring to Handstand Walkover Forward (at end of beam)

From a two-foot running take-off, spring, lifting legs stretched together, with body slightly piked initially, showing counterbalance in

Bent arms.

Insufficient lean of shoulders.

Muscled "press."

Underbalance, inability to raise hips above supports.

Good Technique	Common Technical Errors	Results
forward shoulder lean. Arrive in stretched handstand with fully split legs, and walkover forward to stand on one leg.	Poor stretch in handstand. Insufficient split of legs. Poor flexibility in upper back.	Improper alignment. Lack of amplitude. Lack of fluency.

Forward Walkover (at end of beam) or Tinsica

May be executed from a running one-foot take-off, immediately springing to hands with straight body ascent, passing through handstand in split position, walkover forward.	Too much forward shoulder lean during handspring. No upper back flexibility. All items in 7.8 above.	Wild, jerky, uncontrolled movement. Flat, collapsed walkout.

Turns and Pivots*

The general technique is very similar for all turns and pivots. Each movement must be executed with good alignment of head, shoulders, hips, and weight center over the base of support. Preparation is from a slight knee bend (demiplié). A good body stretch and lift must occur, and the turn must be initiated from within the center of the body, with movement radiating from this central point, with arms, legs, and head following. The arms and free leg (if any) aid the continuous motion, which should have freedom and lightness. The eyes spot a convenient object and focus changes with the degree and rapidity of the turn. With the proper lift, alignment,	Postural difficulties such as stooped body, forward head, sway back, hunched shoulders. Generally poor body stretch, posture, and alignment. Head dropping. Stepping on stiff leg for preparation (exception: pique turn). Uncoordinated arms. *Jump Turns* Poor preparation, take-off, lift, and body stretch in air. *Waltz Turns* Failure to complete half-turn per measure. Lack of supple arm and body movement. Pausing too long before starting or working out of turn.	Lack of lightness and firmness on turn or pivot. Awkward, lacking elegance. Unbalanced turn. Over- or under-turning. Turn incomplete before landing. Heavy landing. Low elevation. Lack of rhythm. Poor coordination. Lack of smooth, fluent transition.

*Refer also to chapter on dance movements.

Good Technique   *Common Technical Errors*   *Results*

stretch, and firmness of control, a
balanced turn looks effortless and
easy. Turns must be performed
with precision of direction, on the
ball of the foot or feet (with a
few exceptions), and with no
dropping of the heel before the
completion of the turn.

7.9   One and One-Half Turn in Lunge or Squat on One Leg

7.10   Arabesque Turn into Scale

7.11   Full Turn Outward in Rear Attitude

Good Technique	Common Technical Errors	Results**

Leaps, Jumps, Hops*

All of these movements must be executed with height in performance, amplitude of upward and/or forward elevation, amplitude, or attainment of full degree of desired body position whether split, stag, tuck, arched, "beat," scissors, cat, etc. Each elevated movement must be preceded by a demi-plié. The body should then lift upward, stretch, and be held firmly in balance throughout the elevation. To be light and soft, the landings should occur into a slightly bent knee to absorb the shock. On both the take-off and landing, the ball of the foot should leave last and contact the beam first. The arms must aid in the elevation and be used to add elegance and grace or "float" to the elevation, especially

Stiff-leggedness, or take-off from flat foot instead of ball of foot.

Loose body; no "set" after take-off.

Incorrect focus.

Poor turn out of hip and leg. Uncoordinated arms and body.

Shoulders lifted during the leap or jump.

Clumsy, awkward.

Insufficient amplitude of body stretch and height on leap.

Disconnected turn with poor rhythm.

Lack of elegance.

Ungainly, heavy execution.

**Refer to errors in turns and pivots.

*Refer also to chapter on dance movements.

7.12   Cat Leap

7.13   Stag or Deer Leap

7.14   Arch Jump, Legs Stretched

Start

7.15   Hitch Kick

Good Technique	Common Technical Errors	Results

if the leap is horizontally forward. All leaps, jumps, and hops must start from a dynamic, forceful movement, show explosive power, and yet look soft and effortless, to land lightly in balance. For horizontal leaps the body must be inclined forward on the take-off.

Flexibilities

Forward Walkover

This is very similar to the floor execution except for the grasp. It is preceded by a controlled extension or preparation kick of the leg and stretch of the body with arms overhead. There is a step forward on one foot and a slight bending of the knee, with placing of hands on the beam. The kick up is as for English handstand, maintaining a full split throughout the inverted position. There is an archover controlled by the upper back. The landing foot is placed close to the hands with a slight bend of the support knee. A push of hips forward occurs and then an immediate return to an upright position, with arms overhead and head and shoulders back until the upright position is reached. The free leg is held high and lowered with control into the following movement. The head remains back throughout the move.	Poor degree of split (less than 180°).	Lack of amplitude and elegance.
	Insufficient flexibility in upper back.	Severe bending on landing leg; bent arms to push off; heavy landing.
	Insufficient inverted body stretch and use of lower back.	Sink in shoulders; lack of elegance and control.
	Twisting body sidewards during turnover.	Loss of balance.
	Lack of thigh strength.	Free leg drops early.
	Switch kick: Insufficient degree of split in both directions.	Lack of amplitude.
	Switch kick not at peak of inverted support.	Poor timing.

Good Technique   *Common Technical Errors*   *Results*

7.16   Forward Walkover

Backward Walkover

This is very similar to the floor execution except for the grasp. Look for a continuous, smooth preparation, head tilted backward with arms moving overhead, back arched, hips pushed forward over support leg, kicking leg lifted high, and a kick over backward as hands contact the beam, showing a full split extension passing through the inverted handstand position. The first foot is placed close to hands, the second leg is stretched as high as possible before the upright position is attained.

Failure to push hips forward.

Use of lower back instead of upper back; poor shoulder extension.

Twisting body slightly during walkover.

Poor degree of split from take-off to landing.

Not stretching into inverted handstand before coming down.

Fall backward too fast; jerky execution; heavy hand contact.

Bent leg kickover; lack of smoothness; lack of elegance.

Out of balance, hand shift in support.

Lacks amplitude.

Bent body "pullover" instead of a stretched walkover.

7.17   Backward Walkover

Good Technique   *Common Technical Errors*   *Results*

Backward Walkover, Stop Handstand, Half-Turn Pirouette, Forward Rollout

The legs are brought together in the inverted stretched support. The weight shifts over the support of the first pivot arm, the other hand regrasps the beam after the one-fourth turn to side handstand with weight over both arms. Repeat weight shift to other arm and one-fourth turn to English to complete the half turn. The pirouette is completed rhythmically and evenly from one stage to the next before the forward roll.

Failure to show control in each stage of the handstand.

Pivots not executed with body weight over support arm.

Poor rhythm, less difficult execution.

Pivoting around the vertical and fall out of balance.

7.18   Backward Walkover Split

Backward Walkover Split

The forward leg must be lowered between the arms and the body must land in perfect control in a deep split.

Poor flexibility forward and insufficient leg split.

Landing in incomplete split and sliding forward to center split near hand grasp.

Handspring Forward on One or Two Arms

Refer to tumbling stunt analysis.

Lack of height and momentary free body position.
Poor timing and lack of sufficient hand and shoulder thrust.

Low amplitude; possible reduction of skill to medium difficulty.
Heavy unbalanced landing.

Good Technique	Common Technical Errors	Results

Flip-Flop (Back Handspring)

Refer to tumbling stunt analysis.

Leaning too far back on take-off, and throwing head first.

Bent arms and/or knees, separation of legs, early hip flexion, heavy hand contact, flat flip-flop.

Taking off with weight forward on balls of feet.

Poor rhythm; too high; hands contact too late; heavy foot contact.

Wheels

Cartwheel

This is very similar to the floor execution with the exception that a slight oblique preparatory position may be assumed instead of a true sideward position. There must be a definite wheel with a 1, 2, 3, 4 rhythmical contact of hand, hand, foot, foot, with the first leg landing closer to the hand than on the floor cartwheel. Take-off is from a slightly bent leg. The body must pass through the stretched inverted side position and return stretched to a good sideward position. The wheel must closely resemble the pure side wheel on the floor.

Kicking into the cartwheel instead of pushing with the bent leg.

Placing hands simultaneously.

Not passing through the vertical.

Maintaining hand grasp too long after first foot contact.

In one-fourth hand pivot:
Pivot not executed during handstand (vertical) phase.
Center of gravity not over base of support during pivot.
Failure to close legs before pivot.

Cartwheel too fast, piking to slow it down.

Poor rhythm.

Pike in hips.

Lack of smoothness and fluency.

Pivot executed while falling out of handstand.
Lack of control and rhythm.

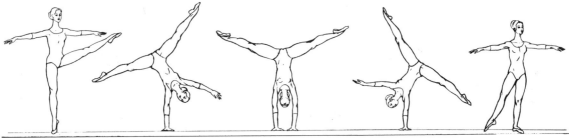

7.19   Cartwheel

Good Technique   *Common Technical Errors*   *Results*

Arab Wheel (Tinsica)

Same as for walkover except that there must be a definite alternate hand placement and rhythmical hand, hand, foot, foot contact. There is a resulting initial twist in the body with one shoulder leading, but the turn forward is over the transverse axis of the body. As the first foot is placed on the beam, the body returns to the oblique until an erect position is attained.	Simultaneous placement of hands.	Changes difficulty to walkover, instead of tinsica.

7.20   Half Cartwheel to One-Fourth Pivot

7.21   One-Arm Cartwheel, Far Arm

Good Technique	*Common Technical Errors*	*Results*

Valdez

Start from a sitting position, with opposite arm and leg extended preferably. The backward turnover should take place over the transverse axis with no twist until the stretched inverted position is reached.

Turning out of line with vertical, not over the transverse axis.

Poor flexibility.

Fall off beam.

Flat or elongated backward movement, awkward.

7.22   Valdez Dismount

Rolls

Forward Roll

From a kneel, squat, lunge, stand, or scale: reach forward with the hands, shift weight to hands as hips are raised, bend elbows (lowering head to the beam), tuck the head between the arms and place the back of the neck and upper back on the beam. The hips move slightly higher, drawing the body into a good pike until the weight settles on the back of the neck and the shoulder area. The hands may or may not (preferably) regrasp under the beam and the elbows

Insufficient hip lift before head placement.

Failure to hold the pike position long enough during roll.

Placing top of head on beam instead of back of neck.

Bent knees.

Failure to keep elbows close to beam.

Fall out of balance, regrasp beam.

Hips drop, stop on back to regain control.

Poor balance and control.

Unattractive.

Unstable, unbalanced roll.
Most errors lead to poor continuity throughout roll.

Good Technique	*Common Technical Errors*	*Results*

remain close to the body. Move forward in a pike with continuity and proceed to the next movement.

Dive Roll

Must show lift, suspension period between take-off and hand contact, and smooth continuous motion throughout roll into following movement.	Hips drop too quickly. Motion too fast.	Jerky, uncoordinated, heavy roll.

7.23   Free Forward Roll (with Dive)

Swing or Whip Roll

Must show good cast, hip elevation, counterbalance forward, complete head tuck, placing back of head on beam, and firm control through inverted pike position into next movement.	Insufficient hip elevation on cast or swing and poor forward shoulder lean.	Early head tuck and roll, heavy head placement, possible bent knees.

7.24   Whip Forward Roll

Good Technique	Common Technical Errors	Results

Backward Roll

With fluency of movement into the back lying position, hands are placed with thumbs preferably on top of the beam under the neck, legs raised, stretched into a pike until hips are over head, leg (or legs) shoots diagonally upward and backward, thumbs push, hands press to side of beam, and body raises in order to free head and arrive in squat, knee scale, etc.

Bent knees.

Stopping before leg shoot.

Poor timing of roll, leg shoot, hand push.

Poor form.

No continuous motion.

Struggle to free head.

—— Start

7.25   Backward Roll to One Foot

Handstands*

Side Handstand

Cartwheel or one-fourth turn into side handstand has good pivot over first support arm, legs are brought together, and body is stretched, showing upward extension with head up. The pause is long enough to show balance and control.

Bending legs or arms.

Poor stretch and alignment.

Weight not over first support arm during one-fourth pivot.

Lack of elegance and control.

Overarch in back and shoulder sag.

Fall out of balance or bending of arms to regain control.

*Refer to squat press and straddle press.

Good Technique	*Common Technical Errors*	*Results*

7.26   Side Handstand

Handstand to Stride Split

Maintain complete forward backward leg split, lean forward, and lower one leg between arm supports to stride support with good 90° split.	Insufficient lean. Insufficient leg split.	Lowering without control. Lack of amplitude.

Handstand to Straddle "L" Hold

The legs are in a wide straddle, the hips are over the shoulders; then the shoulders lean forward over the hands during leg and hip descent for counterbalance, and the legs finish in a straddle "L" support, held at the horizontal.	Insufficient forward lean. Lack of abdominal strength.	Uncontrolled descent: too fast. Legs drop below horizontal during hold.

Handstand to Stoop Through "L" Hold

The legs held firmly together are lowered between the hand supports and are extended horizontally to an "L" position.	Insufficient forward flexibility.	Bent legs on stoop through.

Good Technique	*Common Technical Errors*	*Results*

English Forward Roll

Step onto semi-bent leg, reach out forward placing hands on beam with thumbs together. As weight shifts to hands, kick up into a stretched handstand, with hips, and shoulders over hands, body completely extended, and head up. Show control in English, shift shoulder weight in direction of roll, very slightly pike (moving the center of gravity forward), lower body controlled to beam, tuck head placing back of neck and upper back on beam in front of hands, keep a pike with hips high, and then roll continuously forward into the next movement. Hands may or may not grasp underneath the beam after body contact. Smoothness is essential.

Poor inverted posture.

Passing through inverted support without slight pause.

Lack of arm strength.
Poor timing and rhythm.
Insufficient degree of pike.

Insufficient amplitude in stretch.

Early roll.

Heavy landing on head or back of neck.
Jerky roll-down.
Hips drop early causing lack of fluency and stop in pike.
Repositioning of body in pike position.

7.27 English Handstand Forward Roll   ← *Start*

English Swingdown to Straddle Seat

The shoulders lean forward in front of hands for counterbalance

Too much forward body lean.

Bent arms, overarching.

Good Technique	Common Technical Errors	Results
as the extended body is lowered by a controlled swing to a straddle seat. (Usually followed by a form of a backward roll.)	Insufficient arm strength and control: center of gravity too far behind hands.	Sitting on beam early and rapid swing down, showing poor control through sitting position.

7.28   English Swingdown to Straddle Seat

Backward Roll Extend to Handstand

Refer to tumbling stunt analysis.

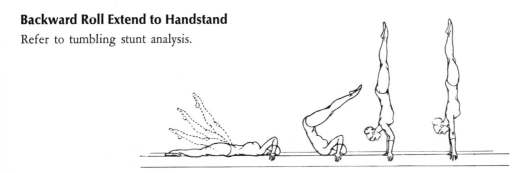

7.29   Backward Roll to Handstand

Dismounts

All landings must be light, supple, and controlled, with no unnecessary arm or trunk movements, no steps or hops, and no turns to hide loss of balance.

Good Technique	*Common Technical Errors*	*Results*

Dismount from Handstand

In general all handstands must show good control in the inverted position before slightly overbalancing into the dismount. The hands and wrists push and the shoulder region forcefully must extend in order to give vitality, life, and explosive character to the finish. The body must straighten up before contacting the mat.

Pivot not performed with weight over the supporting arm.

Poor direction on dismount.

Insufficient straightening of body before landing from stoop or straddle.

Heavy landing, lack of amplitude.

Unbalanced landings, overthrows, undercutting.
Refer to errors in handstands.

Hops, steps, jumps, touches or supports on mat, fall on hips or knees.

7.30   Handstand One-Fourth Turn Dismount

Dismount for Backward or Forward Walkover

The same as for walkovers with the exception that the legs are brought together extended before the stretched descent to landing. There should be a good push-off to show some degree of free position before contact with the mat.

Refer to faults listed under Flexibilities-Walkovers.

Good Technique	*Common Technical Errors*	*Results*

Dismount for Cartwheel

The legs come together in the inverted position. There is a strong push-off with the arm closest to the end of the beam, and free fall with body stretched in a sideward position to a balanced landing with shoulder sideways to beam. The landing is a good distance away from the beam.

Body not passing through vertical.

Maintaining grasp too long: late push-off.

Legs closing too late.

Poor direction on free fall. Piking, awkward appearance.

No "off flight."

Overspin and underbalanced landing.

Dismount for Handspring on One or Both Arms

Look for a good preparatory hurdle, resulting in a good forward handspring emphasizing the rapid and forceful repulsion from the hands. The contact with the hands must be only momentary with the push-off being executed before the body passes the vertical position. The body must lift upward and forward in arched flight before descending to a stand on the mat.

Poor thrust and push-off from support leg and thrust leg.
Poor degree of split and thrust of kicking leg.

Insufficient forward reach with arms.

Poor thrust/repulsion from beam on hands: lack of explosive execution.

Insufficient rotation, lack of amplitude, long flat dismount, possible unbalanced landing.

Shoulders forward, long flat flight, no lift, unbalanced landing.

Low dismount, lack of off-flight, poor body stretch in flight.

Aerials

All aerials must be executed with lift, height, and amplitude (maintaining the correct desired body position in the air), and must land in balance with suppleness. Those movements performed in a series or combined with tumbling movements on the beam must show fluency, continuity, and elegance.

Refer to tumbling skill anaysis for common technical errors and results.

7.31   Gainer with Layout

7.32   Barani

Good Technique	Common Technical Errors	Results

Aerial Walkover, Cartwheel, Barani, Front Somersault

| | Poor "block" with take-off foot; dropping of head and chest into forward lean. | Low flight, no lift. |
| | Too long a step before "block," causing body weight to be too far forward to convert horizontal to vertical force. | Lack of free, light execution with resulting supple, controlled landing. |

Back Tuck Somersault
Refer to tumbling skill analysis.

| | Insufficient upward lift before tucking.
Beginning in off balanced position backward. | Low, whip over somie. |
| | Too much forward lean on take-off. | Slow somersault, incomplete rotation. |

Back Layout Somersault and Full Twisting Somersault
Refer to tumbling skill analysis.

SPECIFIC PENALTIES AND DEDUCTIONS FOR BALANCE BEAM

The specific dimensions of the balance beam are:

Length: 5 meters or 16'5"
Width: 100 mm (upper and lower margins) or 3-15/16"
Height: 120 cm or 47¼"

A Reuther board may be placed on the mat and used for take-off on the mount. The duration of the exercise is from 1 minute 20 seconds to 1 minute 45 seconds. The timer will start the clock (a) at the moment the feet leave the floor or the board for mounts requiring spring or leap movements, and (b) at the moment the hands touch the beam on mounts requiring hand support. Once the hands are placed on the beam the mount must be carried out without a pause. The exercise is terminated the moment the feet of the gymnast contact the floor. A warning signal is given at 1 minute 40 seconds and again at 1 minute 45 seconds. When the second signal is given the gymnast must have dismounted from the beam. She may arrive on the floor after the signal without penalty.

Exercises that are too short are penalized by 0.05 point per second for each second under time.

Exercises that are too long are penalized by 0.3 point. Once the second signal occurs, the judge stops viewing the exercise and evaluates the routine up to that point. A personal deduction under composition of from 0.3 to 0.5 point is taken by each judge for lack of a dismount in addition to the technical deduction taken by the superior judge for overtime.

Deductions for time infractions are taken from the average of the two middle scores by the superior judge.

After a fall to the floor the gymnast must remount the beam within 10 seconds. The clock is kept running during the time she is on the floor and, if she does not remount the beam within this 10-second period, the exercise is finished.

Any number of falls is permitted, each fall being penalized by 0.5 point. After remounting the apparatus the gymnast should not repeat the difficulty or skill missed. It is recommended not to remount the apparatus more than twice. If a first or second fall occurs near the end of the exercise, it is advisable to take this fall as the dismount. The penalty is from 0.3 to 0.5 point for lack of a dismount (sometimes referred to as "dismount too easy" for the exercise) and there is no additional penalty of 0.5 point for the fall.

During the course of an exercise, a gymnast may almost complete the difficult movement and then fall. She receives credit for the difficulty but a deduction for the fall. If she falls during the middle of the movement, she receives no credit for the difficulty and loses 0.5 point for the fall.

No repetitions of either compulsory or optional exercises are allowed unless the head judge agrees to a fault in the apparatus or timing devices.

For both the compulsory and optional exercises an additional approach (balk) is allowed provided the gymnast does not touch the beam or run underneath it. If either of these faults occurs, the penalty is 0.5 point.

Penalties related specifically to the action of the coach and performer are as follows:

Gymnast warms up during a judge's consultation 0.5
Gymnast begins exercise without presentation to superior judge 0.2
Gymnast begins exercise when the red light is on .... No score
Incorrect or inappropriate uniform is worn 0.3
Male coach is in the area of competition (Team penalty unless pre-

viously approved by the decision of meet officials.) 2.0

Coach touches beam 0.2

Coach signals competitor 0.3

Coach speaks to gymnast or vice versa 0.5

Coach walks along side of beam (She may spot only the difficult elements.) 0.3

Coach assists gymnast on dismount after the difficulty is completed or as she arrives on ground 0.5

During poor execution of a dismount, coach assists or catches gymnast before she touches ground 1.5

Coach intentionally touches gymnast, even if very slightly, with little or no aid resulting 1.5

Gymnast intentionally touches coach, even if very slightly, with little or no aid resulting 1.5

Coach or gymnast touches the other unintentionally .... No penalty except that which occurs due to an execution fault.

The remaining penalties can be divided into these groupings:

1. General execution faults: those faults pertaining to corrections in technical execution, amplitude, and general impression.

   a. Small faults: 0.1 to 0.2.

      (1) If the position of the head, hands, or toes is incorrect in one or more important combinations or movements, a 0.1 deduction is made. When such a small fault occurs consistently throughout the exercise, 0.1 cannot be taken each time. The general impression score is then affected by an overall penalty of 0.1 to 0.5. If this small fault is overshadowed by a medium or serious error, the small error is forgotten.
      Example: A larger penalty such as "movement of the arms or legs" to maintain balance is recorded as 0.2.

      (2) A slight straddling of the legs (up to 45°) or bending of the arms, legs, or body 0.2
      Examples: (1) Slight arm bend in handstand. (2) Slight separation of legs on back layout somersault dismount. (3) Slight lean of body right sideward and kick of left leg sideward to maintain balance.

      (3) Each stop (too long a pause) for no apparent reason and each stop beyond the maximum of three times 0.2

(4) Jumps or leaps without amplitude (each time) 0.2
Be familiar with the ideal amplitude for the various leaps and jumps [hitchkick (ciseaux), cabriole, pas de chat, grand jeté, chassé, arch jump, split jump, entrechat] because they all require varying degrees of height to be executed amply and properly.

(5) Turns without sureness (slight loss of balance, hesitation on preparation, or loss of continuity) 0.2

(6) Turns not executed on the ball of the foot and those showing an early drop of the heel 0.2

(7) Monotonous rhythm of a passage (meaning at least a length of the beam) (each time) 0.2

(8) Slight alternate hand placement or delay of one arm over the other as in a knee scale hand position, English hand-stand, etc. 0.1

b. Medium faults: 0.3 to 0.4.

(1) Definite bending of arms, legs, or body or straddling of legs from 45° to 90° 0.3
Example: Obvious and unnecessary movement of the trunk to remain in balance.

(2) Definite lack of amplitude throughout exercise: amplitude not only of leaps and jumps, but of body stretch, posture, leg extension, degree of split, and arm movements 0.3

(3) Supplementary leg support on side of beam in order to maintain balance 0.4

(4) Definite lack of continuity throughout exercise 0.3

(5) Touching beam with hands or fingers in order to remain in balance 0.3
This fault may occur during scale, on low level turn such as one done in lunge position, or on landing from leap. No support is necessary: only slight touch to correct any lack of balance.

c. Serious faults: 0.5 and above.

(1) Support by one hand or both hands on beam for balance 0.5

(2) Overall jerky execution, showing very poor continuity and lack of smooth flow and integration of parts .... 0.5 to 1.0

(3) Fall on apparatus without actually touching floor 0.5

(4) Fall to floor (each time) 0.5

(5) Repetition of element of difficulty that caused fall, or

repetition of difficulty that demonstrated major break without actual fall 0.5

2. Faults specifically related to mounts and dismounts (deductions taken from technical execution).

   a. Touching beam on mount without mounting and then beginning again 0.5

   b. Slight loss of balance on dismount in form of small step or hop 0.1-0.2

   c. Moving 90° left or right to hide loss of balance and equilibrium upon landing 0.2

   d. Landing with torso bent too far forward, without moving feet 0.1

   e. Moving forward with one large step 0.2

   f. Taking one small step forward with no loss of balance 0.1

   g. Moving forward with several steps in order to regain balance 0.5

   h. Falling on knees when landing 0.5

   i. Falling forward onto support of both hands, rearward to support of hips, or against beam 1.0

   j. Lack of dismount (penalty taken from general impression) . 0.3-0.5

3. Faults specifically related to organization, structure, combination, content, and orginality of exercise.

   a. Faults for excess of one type of movement over the other .... Up to 0.5

     Examples:

     (1) Obvious lack of lower level movements such as sitting, lying, kneeling positions .... Up to 0.3

     (2) Over-use of handstand movements (side handstand-straddle "L" hold, side handstand to split (stride) support, English handstand swing down, English handstand forward roll) in same routine without exhibition of other types of difficulties of an inverted nature, such as cartwheels, walkovers, hand pivots, etc. .... Up to 0.5

     (3) Turning in only one direction throughout exercise utilizing half-turns (even though arm movements may differ) at ends of beam .... Up to 0.3

   b. Level of difficulties not up to level of competition .... Up to 0.5

     (1) Omission of one superior difficulty 0.2

     (2) No superior difficulty 0.5

(3) Omission of one or more medium difficulties 0.2

(4) No medium difficulty 0.5

c. Combinations of difficulties and transitions too advanced for gymnast .... Up to 0.5
A gymnast having medium and serious breaks throughout her difficulties or showing pauses and breaks in continuity before and after the more difficult movements and parts, will loose additional points for choosing a composition beyond her performance level.

d. Mount not up to difficulty of routine in general .... Up to 0.2
Example: Using squat-through to rear support mount when other difficulties were, for example, forward and backward walkover, cartwheel-pivot ¼-turn, 1½-lunge turn, two leaps with good amplitude, backward roll extension to handstand, front walkover aerial dismount.

e. Dismount not up to difficulty of routine in general .... Up to 0.3
Example: Handstand walkover mount, full split leap, double turn on half toe, valdez, back tinsica, front walkover on one arm, back roll extension to handstand, one-arm handspring dismount.

f. Using same mount or dismount as prescribed in compulsory exercise 0.3

g. Difficulties not placed progressively throughout routine. Up to 0.5
Gymnasts unsure of difficult movements tend to place the more difficult medium elements or their two superior elements at the end of the routine, demonstrating a lack of courage, preparedness, and risk.
All difficulties in first part of the exercise 0.3

h. Failure to exhibit variety of movements at ends and center of beam, and failure to use entire length advantageously .... Up to 0.5
All difficulties should not be "centered," but should occur throughout the length, including the very ends of the beam.

i. Routine itself (specifically turns, leaps, jumps, hops, combinations of these, and rhythm) not up to level of difficulties. Up to 0.5
Very often the spectacular nature of the superior difficulties takes concentration and awareness away from the remainder of the composition and the gymnast gets away without deductions for performance of a very "stock" routine.

j. Originality of all parts not up to level of competition .... Up to 0.5

(1) Lack of originality in poor routine 0.5

(2) Lack of originality in otherwise good routine 0.2

(3) Stunts and tricks without connectors 0.3

k. An exercise that does not fit the morphology of the gymnast. 0.2-0.4

COMPOSITION AND COACHING HINTS TO INCREASE INDIVIDUAL SCORE

The art of composition for the balance beam exercise is closely related to the method and procedures used in choreographing the particular gymnast's floor exercise.

In the beginning the gymnast learns compulsory exercises suited to her level of accomplishment. As her skill grows she climbs "up the ladder" of compulsory combinations and routines, experiencing many stunts, combinations sequences, and styles. She learns through execution of these prescribed exercises which types and styles of movements she can learn more easily and execute more aesthetically.

Identification of Strengths

She may soon realize that as a result of her explosive power and leg strength, she is an expert leaper and tumbler. Her exercise may exhibit a strong acrobatic or tumbling mount from a running take-off, such as a handspring or an oblique step on mount into an immediate erect position to a balance stand, a moving pass to the end of the beam, or a half or full turn.

Depending on her degree of leg split flexibility, the adept leaper can capitalize on this natural asset and include several of these skills: split jump, arch jump, tuck jump, stag leap, stride leap, scissors leap, or a series of small leaps, hops, and jumps performed with amplitude.

Her routine might include a dive cartwheel, a dive forward roll, or a front or back handspring to demonstrate her tumbling prowess. The final impression would be an aerial tumbling movement of superior character.

The gymnast with exceptional back flexibility, especially in the upper back region, and a good leg split can begin with forward and backward walkovers, developing these into more difficult variations (the tinsica, a one-arm forward or backward walkover, back-walkover to split) and then work to combine these with various hand balances moving in and out of half- and one-fourth-hand pirouettes.

The girl with a sound technical ability in dance can make use of her good carriage and alignment of body segments by combining intricate pivots and turns with a variety of leaps, hops, and jumps. She can contribute dance difficulties, both medium and superior, performed with the elegance and ease so often missing in even highly skilled gymnasts. Her strength lies in her greater body control and extension of the torso and leg. These qualities will enhance the transitions and perhaps the whole exercise. A steadiness, fluency, and beauty of movement will prevail.

Selection and Organization of Content

Each of the types of gymnasts mentioned above should develop a particular area of strength to the utmost, be it explosive power and strength, tumbling ability, body flexibility, or superior dance ability. In addition each gymnast must perfect selected skills in the other categories of movement, so that her routine exemplifies all the necessary elements. She must be careful not to let one type of movement dominate the others.

Once she has defined her strengths and knows her limitations of body structure, she must develop her routine into a composition that is truly her own: one suited to her personality and body type. The resulting composition must be within her capability to execute from beginning to end without traces of fatigue or sloppiness, unnecessary breaks and stops, or a downward trend in amplitude of movement. It is far better to perform a routine with the required number of difficulties than to overload the exercise and so cause fatigue and numerous faults in execution.

The difficulties should be placed throughout the routine; the superior elements must not be crowded into the last section before the dismount. Elements of risk must exist from beginning to end. The difficulties should be an integral part of the whole, just as the transitions and the combinations must correspond to the degree of difficulty of the medium and superior elements.

When choosing difficulties, it is strongly recommended to include at least three passes through the handstand or inverted support position, such as cartwheels, walkovers, tinsicas, and other handstand variations. Such inverted positions are never considered as stops, since the legs are kept moving. It has become necessary to count definitely the stops, handstand, splits, and attitudes that are actually held, to be sure the exercise does not contain more than the maximum number of three.

Acrobatic, tumbling, and dance movements should not be repeated unless in immediate succession. Two front or back walkovers in succession are rated as one superior difficulty if there is no interruption or lengthy pause between executions. If a stop does occur, this constitutes the repetition of a medium difficulty and additional credit is not given.

All walkovers, cartwheels, handstands, etc., must not be placed in the middle of the beam, all turns and pivots should not be near the extremities, and all leaping and jumping movements should not be preceded by a preparatory run or chassé. Variety in the placement of all types of movement in relation to the 16-foot 5-inch length must occur.

All levels and heights must be explored through the fundamental body positions:

lying (front and back), front raised lying support, squatting or half squatting, lunging, inverted, or erect and stretched. The body may assume attitudes with the trunk inclined forward, backward, or sideward. Originality in the presentation of the tuck, pike, and stretched body position may be adapted to the restricting surface of the beam. Movement backward, forward, and sideward with a resulting change of focus adds variety to the content.

It is good to draw from several areas of dance, using modern gymnastics, modern dance, and on occasion folk dance combinations. The dance parts may include elements of jazz, if they are easily integrated, feminine and tastefully performed. The dance movements must not be grossly exaggerated. Exploration of a wide range of arm movements may give new and exciting appearances to ordinary "stock" combinations.

Remember that proper body carriage, posture, and good alignment are foremost. Even the smallest movement must be precise and possess the desired amount of amplitude. Combinations showing erect movement and a raising of the center of gravity through execution on the half-toe are more difficult and more exciting.

Neither dance nor purely acrobatic movement should be predominant. The routine should be an ingenious composition of the many dance elements that combine well with acrobatic and tumbling skills. Movements taken directly from the compulsory exercises will be penalized unless placed in unique and entirely different combinations.

Specific Coaching Hints to Increase Individual Scores

A score of 9.0 points for the execution of a balance beam exercise reflects years of hard work and dedication. How is this achieved? What is the success formula? The specific answer varies for each individual. Coaching must be an individualized program utilizing those particular conditioning exercises, daily training techniques, and motivations that fit the individual. Below are some helpful suggestions for the competitor.

1. Spend a designated period of time on conditioning exercises either each day or on a regular but less frequent basis. Generally, those methods and techniques followed for conditioning and training in the floor exercise event are applicable to the balance beam. Overall flexibility and effortless control are the desired goals. The gymnast must perform specific sets of exercises for improvement and maintenance of leg flexibility, upper back and shoulder flexibility, hip flexibility, and leg strength.

2. Spend time each day on a set of warm-up exercises that emphasize constant brisk movement in an upright posture. The set of warm-ups should take the gymnast from one end of the beam to the other a minimum of

twenty times. Walks, runs, hops, leaps, jumps, gallops, and slides should be included to accomplish:

a. Smoothness and continuity.

b. Elegance in total body posture.

c. Rhythmical variety in execution of the same set of exercises.

d. Varied torso, arms, leg, and head movements within the same set of warm-ups.

e. Full amplitude of all movements.

3. Practice all dance movements and acrobatic and tumbling skills on the floor, progressing to the low beam (six to eight inches higher than the floor) to eliminate the possibility of injury and to enable the spotter to give the necessary hand assists, both for safety and learning purposes. Advance to a beam of mid-level at approximately hip height and then on to the regulation height only when there is complete confidence, correct performance technique, full amplitude, and a 90-percent positive performance record at lower heights.

4. Break down the whole routine into at least four logical sections. Practice each section alone until both sureness and continuity are achieved. Combine two sections and then work halves of routines until there is readiness to perform the routine in its entirety.

5. Perform whole routines from beginning to end without repetition of any missed movements. Work for continuity, rhythm, and sureness. Repeat the routine several times in succession, gradually decreasing the rest interval. Then return to the missed elements and work on each one individually.

6. Practice to music and vary the selections to aid experimentation with rhythm in the warm-up as well as the competitive exercise. Remember that the rhythm of the exercise is extremely important.

7. Mark the beam with chalk at specific points to indicate positions for the more difficult moves. Use chalk or resin on the feet to help stop and stabilize pivots and turns.

8. Occasionally conduct the workout in a competitive atmosphere, following each performance with an evaluation by both the coach and fellow gymnasts.

9. Prior to a competition, remove any movement that does not have a 95 to 100 percent positive performance record. Substitute a mastered skill, even if the difficulty credit is subsequently reduced.

10. Pay particular attention to the physical appearance of the gymnast:

a. Find an attractive hair-do that will remain secure. Add height to the shorter gymnast, if possible, through the hair style. Wear make-up in moderation to complement the naturalness of the gymnast, not to theatrically overpower her.

    b. Minimize structural faults and weight problems by choosing a leotard that will enhance the gymnast's body shape. Pay particular attention to color, degree of leg cut, style of darts, neckline, and sleeve length.

Refer to coaching hints in the dance, floor exercise, and uneven bar chapters. The many helpful theories and suggestions described are also most applicable to the balance beam event.

LIST OF DIFFICULTIES FOR BALANCE BEAM

Mounts

MEDIUM DIFFICULTIES

1. Straddle cut to rear support.
2. Wolf mount with 1 or 1½ turn.
3. Scissors mount—½ turn to a free position of balance.
4. Headstand.
5. Oblique free foot mount to 1 foot or to squat position with ½ or full turn (see figure 7-6).
6. Free foot mount on end of beam on one foot with other leg free.
7. Same as No. 6 with turn.
8. Forward roll on end of beam finishing in stand on one foot (see fig. 7-3).
9. Forward roll to one foot rising up into front scale.
10. Jump onto beam with one foot, grasping manually, stretch arms and support leg and swing other leg to vertical split or needle scale.
11. Handstand press from stoop or squat mount.
12. Shoulder stand on one shoulder (on end or at side) (see figure 7-5).
13. Jump to straddle split (Japanese split).
14. Jump to knee scale and full turn (at end of beam).

SUPERIOR DIFFICULTIES

1. On end of beam roll forward arriving on one leg and swing legs alternately to handstand.
2. Free foot mount on end of beam on one foot followed by jump ½ turn on one leg ending in upright standing position.
3. Like No. 2, but finish in squat (crouched) position after jump ½ turn.

4. Oblique mount onto one foot to front scale.
5. Oblique mount to front scale directly at the side of the beam, facing out.
6. On end of beam hold a straddle and press up to handstand (see fig. 7-2).
7. Same as No. 6 but in middle of beam.
8. Jump with spring to handstand with legs together or straddled on end or in middle of beam.
9. Jump with a straight body to handstand walkover out on end of beam (see figure 7-8).
10. Thief vault mount to rear support (see figure 7-7).
11. Spring to shoulder stand, roll over shoulder, finish with a half turn to free sitting position.
12. Jump on end of beam into side cartwheel.
13. Jump on end of beam with tinsica.

Turns and Pivots

MEDIUM DIFFICULTIES

1. One full turn on one leg in erect stand.
2. Complete one turn in squat stand on one leg without hand support (see figure 7-9).
3. Standing on one leg, execute 1½ turn descending to squat stand.
4. From stand on one leg (the other leg bent in front or back), complete one turn and stretch bent leg backward into front scale.
5. From stand on one leg complete minimum of one turn to balance on one leg (see figure 7-10).
6. Full turn inward with step.
7. Full turn outward with step (see figure 7-11).
8. From a stand on one leg with foot of free leg against support leg, complete a minimum of 1½ turns.
9. Jump from both feet with minimum of ½ turn.
10. Waltz turns with a minimum of ½ turn per 3 beats.

SUPERIOR DIFFICULTIES

1. Jump from both feet and complete full turn.
2. Two continuous turns in same level.
3. 1½ turn on one knee.
4. Full turn followed by full camel turn to split; illusion-full camel turn-split; or illusion to split.
5. Leap onto one leg and 1½ turn to front scale.

6. Cat leap with ½ turn.
7. English handstand: ½-pirouette turn in waltz rhythm.

Leaps and Jumps

MEDIUM DIFFICULTIES

1. Several hops or jumps in succession with changing of position of legs. *Example:* hop left with right leg in rear attitude, hop left with right leg extended forward, step right, "push leap" right, land right, leap forward left to squat-stand.
2. Large cat leap showing amplitude (see figure 7-12).
3. Deer leap or stag leap with front knee bent (see figure 7-13).
4. Arched jump, with legs together and stretched (see figure 7-14).
5. Arched jump with bending of two legs, heels lifted backward (cheerleader jump).
6. Arch jump with one leg bent in rear and other straight.
7. Hitchkick or scissors forward followed by hitchkick or scissors backward (see figure 7-15).
8. Stag split leap.
9. Stride leap with scissors or changing of leg (sweeping split).
10. Turning jump or leap (½ turn).
11. Turning leap (½ turn) arriving in squat, followed by full turn in squat.
12. Split jump from both feet.
13. Leap with "beat" of legs forward (cabriole).
14. Leap with "beat" of legs backward (cabriole).
15. Leap with "beat" of legs sideward (cabriole).

SUPERIOR DIFFICULTIES

1. Squat jump or tuck jump (knees forward) with ½ turn.
2. Stag leap with ½ turn.
3. Scissors leap with ½ turn.
4. Leap or jump with ½ turn to scale or needle scale.
5. Gallop step rapidly with ½ turn each time.
6. Several waltz turning jumps in succession (½ turns each time).
7. Cat leap with ½ turn.
8. Swing one leg forward, ½ turning leap on support leg (battement tourne with large hop).
9. Series of large leaps, jumps (different or similar). *Example:* back hitchkick, front cabriole, cat leap, stride leap in succession with amplitude.
10. ½ turning jump, like butterfly, in horizontal plane.

Flexibilities

MEDIUM DIFFICULTIES

1. Forward walkover (see figure 7-16).
2. Backward walkover (see figure 7-17).
3. Backward walkover with switch leg landing on same foot as take-off.
4. Turnover forward or backward,* arriving on one leg and, without stop, returning to starting position.
5. Turnover backward, stopping in stag handstand.
6. Turnover backward, rolling onto chest, flexing arms.

SUPERIOR DIFFICULTIES

1. Series of walkovers (two or more forward or backward).
2. Walkover forward on one hand.
3. Walkover backward on one hand.
4. Backward limber** with legs together, arriving on knees.
5. Turnover backward, stopping in handstand, ½-turn pirouette and forward roll out of handstand.
6. Turnover backward, momentarily stop handstand, ½-turn pirouette "press" down finishing in free straddle support or "V" sit.
7. Turnover backward to momentarily controlled handstand, ¼ turn to side handstand, lower to side split.
8. Handspring forward.
9. Handspring forward on one arm.
10. Aerial walkover.
11. Back handspring (onto one or two legs).

Wheels

MEDIUM DIFFICULTIES

1. Cartwheel (wheel sidewards) (see figure 7-19).
2. Cartwheel ¼ turn outward in direction of wheel.
3. Cartwheel from a squat or sit.
4. ½ cartwheel to straddled side handstand, ¼ pivot turn on hands (end facing initial direction).
5. ½ cartwheel, with more than ¼ pivot on hands (see figure 7-20).

SUPERIOR DIFFICULTIES

1. Valdez: tinsica backwards starting from a crouched position (see figure

---

*Turnover backward is half back walkover to hand support position.

**Backward limber is continuous backward movement through hand support with legs together throughout.

7-22). (As dismount, medium difficulty.)

2. Tinsica, forward and then backward.
3. Dive cartwheel or tinsica.
4. Aerial cartwheel.
5. Cartwheel on far arm (see figure 7-21).
6. Backward cartwheel with ¼ turn into side cartwheel.
7. Successive cartwheels (2 or more on 2 arms or 1).

Rolls

MEDIUM DIFFICULTIES

1. Roll forward without stopping with balance and continuity.
2. Dive roll.
3. Headstand, forward roll.
4. Shoulder stand roll forward, coming up quickly.
5. Roll forward from two feet, followed by walkover forward.
6. From cross straddle support, swing or whip forward roll (see figure 7-24).
7. Roll backward over the head to one or two feet, starting in squat or crouched position (see figure 7-25).

SUPERIOR DIFFICULTIES

1. Free roll forward, without support of hands (see figure 7-23).

Inverted Supports, Handstands

(See figures 7-26, 7-27 and 7-28.)

MEDIUM DIFFICULTIES

1. Side handstand and split outside arms.
2. Handstand, forward roll, and without stopping thrust one leg backward to front split.
3. Side handstand, descend to straddle "L" hold.

SUPERIOR DIFFICULTIES

1. Handstand, forward roll (release hands upon initial head contact).
2. Roll backward, extend to handstand (see figure 7-29).
3. Roll backward, extend and ¼ turn to side handstand.
4. Handstand (side), lower with legs straddled to straddle "L" hold and return press to stretched handstand.

Dismounts

MEDIUM DIFFICULTIES

1. Side handstand, ¼ or ½ turn (see figure 7-30).

2. Side handstand, ¼ turn, cartwheel.
3. Side handstand stoop.
4. Side handstand straddle cut-off.
5. Backwalkover.
6. Forward turnover or walkover.
7. Backward or forward walkover on one arm.
8. Cartwheel at end of beam with turn.
9. Cartwheel at side of beam with turn.
10. Cartwheel on one arm (near arm).
11. Cartwheel on one arm (far arm).
12. Slowly press up into handstand with legs stretched or straddled and turn over to stand.
13. Handspring.
14. Handspring with support on one arm.
15. Backward tinsica.
16. Forward tinsica.
17. Tinsica with turn.
18. Not listed by FIG: Valdez dismount (see figure 7-22).

SUPERIOR DIFFICULTIES

1. Front tuck somersault from stand on two feet, from sidestand.
2. Back tuck somersault from stand on two feet, from sidestand.
3. Layout somersault backward from stand on two feet—at end of beam.
4. Layout with twist from stand on two feet—at end of beam.
5. Running take-off on one foot, piked somersault forward.
6. Run forward, take-off on one foot, and stretched somersault forward.
7. Run forward, spring from one foot and stretched somersault forward with ½ or full twist.
8. Gainer (thrust from one foot, back somie, while moving forward) (see figure 7-31).
9. Back handspring at end of beam.
10. Back handspring at side of beam.
11. From upright stand facing sidewards on beam, thrust or take off on one leg and somersault forward (front aerial off the side).
12. Run, roundoff, back handspring.
13. Run, roundoff, tuck somersault backward.
14. Run, roundoff, layout somersault backward.
15. Run, roundoff, somersault with ½ or full twist.
16. Aerial cartwheel.
17. Aerial cartwheel with ¼, ½, or full turn (see figure 7-32). (Barani is placed in this classification.)

8

Uneven Parallel Bars

ANDREA BODO SCHMID

INTRODUCTION

The exercises performed on the uneven parallel bars are primarily swinging, circling, and kipping movements, with releases and regrasps used as the performer changes from bar to bar. Support exercises, stands, seats, and static positions should be used only as temporary or passing positions. Two short stops are permitted in each routine for momentary positions of balance or as transitions to very difficult elements.

In modern routines the individual elements are linked without unjustified stops. The emphasis is on uninterrupted swinging, the changing of directions, and releases from bar to bar. An exercise should show lightness, assurance, and good form. The achievement of a continuous flow of movement and correct form is based on mechanical principles. Therefore, a thorough understanding of mechanical principles is essential for teachers, coaches, and judges.

This chapter provides information on correct form in uneven parallel bars movements and on combinations insuring uninterrupted graceful exercise when the gymnast has mastered her technique. The chapter will also enable the judge to recognize deviations instantly and so make the proper deductions.

MECHANICAL PRINCIPLES UTILIZED IN UNEVEN BARS MOVEMENTS
Conservation of Angular Momentum

The principle of conservation of angular momentum has almost continuous application in uneven bars

stunts. A teacher who understands and can recognize it will be able to give more effective coaching advice. Knowledge of the principle is equally valuable to a gymnast, since by comprehending its application she can perform movements in a more effortless and graceful manner.

This principle can be clearly demonstrated with a weight attached to a string tied over the low bar. If the weight is lifted up to the right side of the bar and let go, it will swing like a pendulum and will rise on the left side to about the same height as that from which it was released on the right. If the action is repeated but the radius of rotation is reduced by pulling the string when the weight passes under the bar, the weight will rise higher on the left side than its point of release on the right, and it may even circle around the bar. By reducing the radius of rotation one decreases the moment of inertia* of the swinging weight but increases the angular velocity (speed of rotation). Pulling the string actually increases the kinetic energy of the pendulum; consequently, the weight rises higher. The gymnast uses the same principle working on the bar.

In any circling movement on the uneven bars (for example, hip circles) the radius of rotation should be lengthened on the downswing and shortened on the upswing to increase the speed of rotation.

At the point when the center of gravity passes di-

*Moment of inertia in rotational motion is analogous to mass (inertia) in straight motion.

8.1   Backward Hip Circle

Preparation Swing   (Cast)

Downswing   Body extended to increase radius of rotation.

Upswing   Body slightly piked (arms could be flexed but this is considered poor form) to shorten the radius of rotation.

Finishing Position   Body opens up to stop rotation.

rectly under the bar, the momentum gained by the downswing (due to gravity) must be conserved by shortening the radius of rotation. This speeds up the rotation, so that the circle may be completed. For example, in a backward hip circle (see figure 8-1) as the movement starts, the body should be elongated to increase the radius of rotation in the downswing. As the legs pass directly under the hands, the hips should be slightly flexed, to shorten the radius of rotation

on the upswing and thereby increase the angular velocity. At completion of the circle, the gymnast extends her body, whereupon her angular velocity is greatly decreased and she stops, ready to continue her exercise. The same principle applies to knee circles, seat circles, sole circles, and back hip pullovers.

Kipping movements from a glide also necessitate application of this principle. (See figure 8-2.) In this exercise the performer swings her body back and forth

8.2   Glide Kip

Preparation Swing

Upswing   Body piked to shorten radius slightly.

Downswing   Body extended to place center of gravity nearer to hands (center of rotation).

Finishing Position   Ready to swing legs to continue with any other movement.

by alternate trunk flexion and trunk extension to gain momentum. On the upswing the radius of rotation is shortened by hip flexion. This helps to overcome gravitational force and gives the performer angular acceleration upward. During the pike the back muscles and the hamstring muscles are stretched to prepare for a vigorous extension of the hip joint on the downswing. This action brings the body upward, placing the center of gravity nearer to the center of rotation to the bar. The glide kip is a complex movement: the performer must shorten the radius of rotation considerably by swinging her legs at the proper time and bringing her center of gravity to the bar.

If the gymnast performs a twisting movement she employs the principle of conservation of angular momentum around her longitudinal axis. In a hecht over low bar with full twist, for example, the gymnast wants to rotate around her longitudinal axis. As the hecht has been initiated coming out of piked position to a stretched position, the performer twists her head, shoulder, and chest to the right and throws her left arm across to her right shoulder (if the twisting is to the right). As the twist has been started, the gymnast folds her arm across her chest. This action shortens the radius of rotation and increases the angular velocity of the twist. At the termination of the twist both

8.3 Forward Somersault Dismount

Preparation Swing Arms nearly vertical, center of gravity higher than point of support.

Somersault Body in tuck position to increase velocity of rotation.

Landing Arms and body extended to stop angular velocity.

arms are extended sideward to increase the moment of inertia and to stop the rotation so that controlled landing may be achieved.

Another example of the use of conservation of angular momentum is found in the forward somersault dismount. The gymnast starts the movement from a front support on the high bar, facing the low bar. The legs are swung forward to initiate a high backward swing (cast). The arms are extended in a nearly vertical position. When her body is slightly above the horizontal position, she drives her hips upward (pikes) and simultaneously releases the bar, tucks tightly, and pulls her head forward down to her knees to somersault (that is, to increase the rotation around her center of gravity). The gymnast gains her initial rotation by the swing, heel movement, and hip lift. The velocity of her rotation at the beginning is moderate, but as soon as she is in the air she draws her arms and legs closer to the center of gravity of her body (tuck position) in order to shorten her radius of rotation and thereby increase her velocity of rotation. At the completion of the somersault she extends her body and arms, whereupon her angular velocity decreases greatly so that controlled landing may be achieved. (See figure 8-3.)

It should be noted that timing is most important in any movement in which the conservation of angular momentum is applied.

Law of Inertia

At rest the body tends to resist being set into motion. When in motion, however, the body tends to remain in motion at a constant speed until another force stops it (Newton's First Law). In straight motion the resistance of the body is proportional to its mass. In rotational motion the resistance of the body to any change in its angular velocity is the moment of inertia of the body.

This principle is applied to all somersaults and twisting and circling movements. When rotation has been initiated it can be stopped only by another force. Therefore, to decrease the velocity of rotation, the gymnast lengthens the radius of rotation by (a) extending her body in circling movements and somersaults or (b) extending her arms in twisting moves to slow down. (See figures 8-1 and 8-3.)

Law of Reaction

The principle, "To every action there is an equal and opposite reaction" (Newton's Third Law), applies to all motion. Motion in gymnastics can be produced only when force has been applied to the body. In movements on the uneven parallel bars, the gymnast applies force to the bar. The counteraction of the bar pushes back and reacts on the gymnast. For example, in a cast a gymnast pushes down and forward on the bar, which then resists the force and pushes the body up and backward. This reaction, or counterforce, enables the gymnast to perform a free front support position. (See figure 8-4.)

Since the bar is flexible, it acts as a spring. When a force is acting upon the bar it will bend down until its reacting force is equal to the acting force of the gymnast. Larger deflection will give larger reaction force. This can be clearly observed when the gymnast performs a straddle jump backward over the high bar to a long hang. (See figure 8-22.) She bends her knees quickly and lets her body accelerate downward as the result of gravitational force. She deflects the low bar, on which she is standing, and then suddenly straightens her legs, exerting a lifting force. Simultaneously the bar straightens and projects the gymnast into the air. The reaction force of the bar and the muscular force of the gymnast are additive, since they are in the same upward direction. (The functions of the action-reaction and spring forces described here are simplified for easier understanding.)

This action-reaction principle also holds true for the mid-air movements of parts of the gymnast's body. If the gymnast is in the air, free from any support,

Floor Line

$$F_1 = F_2$$

8.4   Action and Reaction

The body exerts a force on the bar (action). The bar in turn exerts a force on the
body which is equal in magnitude and opposite in direction (reaction).

her body movements will not raise or lower her center
of gravity, but she may raise, lower, or rotate parts
of her body around her center of gravity and simultaneously produce similar but opposite motions with
the other parts of her body by the use of internal
muscular force. For instance, in the straddle jump
backward over the high bar to a long hang (see figure 8-22), when the gymnast is in the air she lifts
her legs upward to clear the high bar. To remain in
the correct position she must obey the action-reaction
principle and she must bend her upper body forward.
Actually she applies the same but opposite angular
displacement to her legs as to her upper body, around
the transverse axis which runs from one side of her
body to the other side through her center of gravity
in the area of her hips. The forward somersault dismount also provides a good illustration of this principle. (See figure 8-3.) The height to which the
performer lifts her hips in the preparation swing de-

termines the height of the dismount. This is because
she is unable to raise her center of weight higher while
unsupported in the air, but during the flight and
rotation she is able to tuck around her transverse axis
to speed up the rotation. Tucking actually refers to
opposing movements of the head (also chest and
arms) and knees (also thighs and legs): the head is
moved down and the knees are moved up at the same
angle and brought together by internal muscular force.
At the end of the somersault the gymnast moves her
head up and knees down at the same angle to open
up her body. Thus in the air the chest and the thighs
are pivoted about the transverse axis to the same degree but in opposite directions.

Balance

In all arm support movements, the center of gravity
of the body should be above the point of support.

Weightlessness

In all swinging movements, at the end of the swing, when the momentum resulting from the swing and that from the gravitational pull become equal, there is a moment of weightlessness. At this moment the gymnast can change easily to the succeeding movement. Thus releases and regrasps are normally performed at this moment.

Summation of Forces

The summation of forces may take place in a given direction if the forces are added successively at the point of the greatest velocity and with no hesitation. Thus, for example, any stunt that necessitates pulling the body up and then pushing it further upward should be performed without pause. The pulling and pushing forces should be added to one another. Most of the force comes, in fact, from the sequential contraction of the muscles, which must be timed precisely.

The principle of the summation of forces together with the value of proper timing can be observed in a KIP. In this movement it is necessary to pull the body up and then push it further upward. (See figure 8-2.) The complete movement can be performed only if there is no hesitation between the pull and the push. Although there is some overlapping in the joint actions, they tend to take place sequentially, starting with the hips, then the shoulders, next the elbows, and terminating at the hands.

An application of the sequential principle is seen in all take-offs for mounts as well. First the arms swing upward, then the hips extend, next the knees extend, and finally the feet push against the mat or Reuther board. Each succeeding movement has begun before the preceding one has been completed. The spring force of the Reuther board acts on the gymnast also, projecting her into the air.

ANALYSIS OF SELECTED UNEVEN BARS MOVEMENTS

Uneven bars movements are so numerous that it is impossible to analyze each. The movements selected for analysis here are representative and chosen so that gymnasts, teachers, and judges can analyze similar movements on their own.

Good Technique	*Common Technical Errors*	*Results*
Backward Hip Circle		
High cast; straight body only a slight pike as hips contact bar; arms straight throughout move; smooth, controlled circle; finish in straight arm support position (see figure 8-1).	Piking too soon.	Practically impossible to carry out movement, or very jerky execution.
	Throwing head back before hips contact bar.	
	Not keeping hips close to bar.	Jerky execution; unattractive.
	Not rotating hands around bar.	Jerky execution; unattractive.
	Bent arms.	Unattractive.
	Rounding upper back; not extending body when coming out of hip circle.	Unattractive; lack of control; continuation of circle.

Good Technique	*Common Technical Errors*	*Results*

Poor

Good

8.5   Forward Seat Circle, Catch High Bar

Poor   Sitting on bar; knees not in line with hands.
Body touching bar throughout circle; coming up by arching body.

Good   Hips lifted high, knees in line with hands.
Body free of bar and piked.
Return to near-free "V" seat.
Finishing position.

Forward Seat Circle, Catching High Bar

Weight on hands; arms straight; hips lifted high and knees in line with hands at beginning of stunt; body in piked position; return to near-free "V" seat before opening body to catch high bar; smooth, controlled execution (see figure 8-5).	Not lifting hips high. Not keeping body away from bar. Slightly bent arms.	Falling off; circle not completed; poor seat circle; rotation too slow; unattractive.

Good Technique	Common Technical Errors	Results
	Coming up to sitting position by extending body too early.	
	Not rotating hands around bar.	Lack of control.
	Reaching for bar too soon. Not looking for high bar. Body not extended at end of move.	

Cast to Squat-Through

Good Technique	Common Technical Errors	Results
High cast; body extended; shoulders forward; legs together (easy to combine with other movements).	Insufficient height on cast.	Jerky execution; too fast.
	Legs bending too early.	
	Insufficient forward lean and tuck.	Lack of control; touching bars on squat-through; unattractive.
	Body arched in cast; head back (not in line with body).	Low cast; unable to get legs through.

Flying Hip Circle

Good Technique	Common Technical Errors	Results
High cast with straight arms; body fully extended in cast and swing; cast with arms near vertical, fluent movement into extended body position; smooth transition to hip circle; ability to control speed of hip circle and lift upper body into front support position.	Body arched in cast.	Too much speed in hip circle.
	Cast too low.	Jerky execution; lack of amplitude; unattractive; too slow.
	Cast with bent arms.	Practically impossible to circle, or very jerky execution; hips fall away from low bar.
	Body not fully extended in cast. Piking before contacting low bar. Releasing high bar too soon. Releasing high bar too late. Not keeping hips close to bar.	Jerky execution; unattractive; lack of control.

Good Technique	Common Technical Errors	Results

Not rotating hands around bar.

Rounding upper back, not extending and lifting upper body as coming out of hip circle.

Poor

Good

8.6   Underswing Half-Turn

Poor   Arms slightly bent as body drops back.
Legs too far from bar.
Body not extended parallel to floor and piking during turn.
Body piking after turn.

Good   Arms straight, legs lifted upward, and thighs close to bar.
Body extended and parallel to floor at end of turn.
Body extended after turn.

Underswing Half-Turn to Long Hang

Arms straight throughout move; high swing; body fully extended	Bending arms, not dropping back from shoulders.	Jerky execution; underswing too low; unattractive.

Good Technique	Common Technical Errors	Results
at end of turn; turn completed before downswing begins; smooth grip change (see figure 8-6).	Not lifting legs upward and not keeping thighs close to bar until shoulders pass under bar.	
	Not twisting into extension at height of underswing.	Bad direction of legs; legs bent; legs separated; changing grip too soon or too late; turning too early or too late; jerky execution; hard to control; unattractive.
	Insufficient cast and leg thrust under bar.	
	Turn not completed during height of underswing.	
	Body not extended and parallel to floor at end of turn.	
	Body bent after turn.	Momentum lost; hard to combine with other move.

Glide Kip

Forward glide performed with feet a few inches off mat; after reaching full extension position, body pikes sharply; ankles are lifted to bars; legs are lifted upward until bar is at hip level, then swung outward and downward, pushing down with arms and rotating grips to finish in front support position; effortless, fluid execution of kip with arms straight throughout move (easy to combine with other movements) (see figure 8-2).	Not lifting hips back enough at beginning of glide.	Lack of continuity; jerky execution; arms bent and hips move away from bar; hard to combine with next move.
	Body not extended at end of glide.	
	Lifting legs too soon or too late to bar.	
	Not helping with arms and rotating grip slightly.	
	Not lifting legs upward until bar is at hip level.	Lack of fluidity; bent arms; hips fall away from bar on rise, resulting in kip to chest rather than to good front support position.

Good Technique	Common Technical Errors	Results

Hecht Dismount

High cast with straight arms; smooth transition to hip circle; noticeable lift of upper body upward and forward; body arched and legs straight from popping off to landing.

Poor cast and hip circle (see flying hip circle).

Not lifting head, arms, and upper body forcefully upward and forward.

Lifting too soon or too late.

Not arching body after popping off bar.

Bent legs.

Unattractive; not enough momentum for high hecht dismount.

Lack of control; unattractive; inability to keep body extended during suspension before landing; low hecht; poor landing.

Poor style.

UNEVEN BARS MEASUREMENTS

The measurements of the uneven parallel bars for competition should be as follows:

Height of high bar: 2.30 meters (7'6½")
Height of low bar: 1.50 meters (4'11")
Width of space between two bars: 54 to 78 cm approximately (1'8" to 2'3")
Bar shape: oval: 42 mm top width (1.65"), 36 mm bottom width (1.41"),
   48 mm length from top to bottom (1.88")

Only the low bar may be adjusted inward or outward, within the regulation distance (54 to 78 cm), to suit the gymnast.

PENALTIES AND DEDUCTIONS

There is no time limit for the performance on uneven parallel bars in competition. The exercise should contain four medium and two superior difficulties and approximately twelve to fourteen movements. More difficulties and moves are allowed but recommended only if the gymnast can perform her routine with proper technique and good execution.

Penalties specifically related to actions of the coach and performer are as follows:

Action	Penalty (points)
1. Coach touching bars	0.2
2. Coach giving signals to gymnast	0.3
3. Coach speaking to gymnast	0.5
4. Coach standing between bars	0.5
5. Coach's aid during the exercise (even for light touch)	1.5
6. Coach's aid on dismount after arriving on mat	0.5
7. Warming up on bars during judges' consultation	0.5

As indicated above, the coach is allowed to be present to prevent accidents as long as she neither touches the gymnast nor helps her in the execution of her routine. In addition, the coach may not position herself between the bars or obstruct the view of the judges. In no case during the competition may the coach or any other person talk or signal to the gymnast while she is executing her routine.

Mount

The use of the Reuther springboard is authorized on the mat for mount. A supplementary run and take-off for the mount is authorized provided that the gymnast does not touch the apparatus or run underneath it. If the gymnast touches a bar or runs underneath the bars, she may repeat her mount or continue her exercise with a penalty of 1.0 point.

Composition

In the uneven bars routine, the individual elements are logically linked without unjustified stops. The movements must be continuous and should not be interrupted. An interruption is penalized. For example, if when executing a kip from low bar to high bar (stationary kip) and squat-through to the rear support a gymnast pauses between the elements or makes an extra swing before the squat-through, this is considered an interruption, for which the penalty is 0.3 point (0.2 point for stop without reason and 0.1 point for lack of continuity). It should be noted that this type of error is not considered an extra swing (which has a penalty 0.5 point, as listed in the FIG Code of Points). This is because the stationary kip can be finished in a front support position on the high bar and the gymnast does the "extra swing" only to execute another movement: in this case the squat-through to rear support. However, if a gymnast performs, for example, an eagle catch, single leg shootover, mill or stride circle regrasp high bar, and does an extra swing before raising one leg over the low bar, the penalty is 0.5 point because the eagle catch should be finished in a full arch at the moment of grasp on the high bar and the next skill (single leg shootover) should start from this position: there is no need for an extra swing to initiate this movement.

There should be a continuous flow of movement in the routine. Two short stops are permitted for momentary balance or as transitions to difficult elements. Stops in excess of this are penalized by 0.2 point each. For example, if the contestant performs a stoop through to a back seat circle and pauses between these two elements, the penalty is 0.2 point. It should be noted that deductions for discontinuity (breaks, stops, etc.) are to be taken from the areas of execution, amplitude, and general impression, and not from composition.

Excessive repetitions of a movement, such as the straddle glide kip or the same circling movement, must be avoided. Difficult elements should be distributed throughout the routine. Failure to do so can result in a penalty up to 0.5 point.

The mount and dismount should be in harmony with the rest of the exercise. The penalty for a mount which is too simple or a dismount which is out of character with the rest of the routine is from 0.1 to 0.5 point. For using the same mount or dismount as in the compulsory exercise, there is a penalty of 0.3 point. Dismounts must be from manual support or body support. A dismount by somersault from a stand on the bar is not permitted and is penalized by 0.5 point.

Execution

A perfect exercise is one that is presented with elegance, ease, and sureness, and in good rhythm, with no faults in execution. Specific penalties for execution are listed below (see also general faults in chapter 3):

Action	Penalty (points)
1. Touching bar or mat lightly with feet	0.1

Example: cast to squat-through—feet lightly touch bar at squat-through.

2. Touching bar or mat heavily with feet	0.2

Example: glide kip—when gliding out, gymnast touches mat with noise.

3. Placing weight on feet on mat during glide or any movement	1.0

Example: glide kip—during downswing phase (see figure 8-2) gymnast puts feet on mat to help herself up to front support position.

4. Alternate hand grasp when not justified	0.2

Example: Forward seat circle, catch high bar, end in rear lying position—gymnast grasps high bar with one hand first then with the other, when it should be grasped simultaneously with both hands.

5. Support of one hand against bar	0.5

Example: From front support on low bar, facing high bar, cast to backward stoop sole circle—contestant loses balance at stoop and with support of one hand against high bar regains balance and continues with backward stoop sole circle.

6. Hang with one hand before regaining high bar without supplementary support 0.5
Exampe: Eagle catch—performer pops off low bar to catch high bar in eagle grip, loses grip with one hand, but then reaches again and recovers without help from feet.

7. Hang with one hand before regaining high bar with supplementary support 1.0
Example: Eagle catch—performer has same problem as above in No. 6, but can regain grip only by touching low bar with feet. (It should be noted that this is considered a fall on the apparatus and as such penalized by 1.0 point.)

Falls

Any fall is penalized by 1.0 point, provided the contestant remounts and continues her routine. If any interruption lasts more than 30 seconds, the exercise is considered terminated. The 30 seconds may be utilized by the gymnast for adjusting a handguard and/or using magnesium. After remounting the apparatus the gymnast should not repeat the movement she missed, or she will be penalized (for repeating a missed element of difficulty) by 0.5 point.

If the gymnast falls when she has nearly completed the difficult movement, she will receive credit for the difficulty; however, if she falls during the middle of the movement, she will get no credit. If when the gymnast falls the coach touches her to recover her balance, there is a deduction of 1.5 points but no additional penalty for the fall.

Dismounts

Landing must be done with elegance and sureness. For an exercise which does not end with good posture, the deductions are as follows:

Action	*Penalty (points)*
1. Unnecessary body movement in order to maintain balance	0.1-0.2
2. Small step or hop	0.1-0.2
3. Several steps or hops	0.5
4. Touching mat with hands	0.5
5. Falling on knees without placing hands on mat	0.5
6. Falling on hips or knees while placing weight on hands	1.0

COMPOSITION FOR ROUTINE
Theory of Composition

The basic elements of an uneven parallel bars routine must be included in the exercise to insure an appropriate and correct composition. Consequently, the routine on the uneven bars should include a mount, swinging movements, circling movements, kipping movements, releases and regrasps, and a dismount. A contestant may have a very difficult routine, but without the required elements the routine will incur a penalty. For example, if the exercise lacks a circling movement around the hand grasps (seat circle, sole circle, etc.), there will be a penalty of 0.2 point.

The composition of the optional routine must differ clearly from that of the compulsory exercise, especially in the mount and dismount. Including movements or connecting elements from the compulsory routine does not necessarily constitute a fault in the composition, if the combinations before and after these elements are different.

The exercise should contain four medium and two superior difficulties and approximately twelve to fourteen movements. It is unwise to perform a greater number of difficulties and moves than required unless the amplitude and form are of high standard. Too many difficulties cause the gymnast to tire, make more technical and execution errors, and so receive a lower score. The difficulty of elements should be progressive throughout the routine. The difficulty of the mount and dismount should be in harmony with the rest of the exercise.

Strength movements are not acceptable. Of course, most uneven bars moves require strength; they must not be performed, however, with a *show* of strength. For example, when a gymnast shows strain in performing a forward hip circle to a handstand, there will be a deduction. However, if the movement is executed with the illusion of effortless ease, no deduction will be given.

The composition must also show creativity and versatility, since credit is given for originality. Versatility can be shown in the gymnast's use of different types of movement combinations and movements in different directions as well as over and under the high and low bars. Repetition of the same movement or type of movement (for example, kipping movements) is penalized as poor composition. Top gymnasts show from four to seven release moves and some twisting movements to make their routine interesting to watch. Modern routines often appear shorter, for they place elements of high difficulty back to back to create new connecting moves. An original and difficult routine executed with small mistakes will get more points than an exercise which is stereotyped but perfectly performed.

Theory of Combination

In addition to originality and difficulty, a good routine must show correct technique, good form, and smoothness of composition. This can be facilitated by a proper combination of movements.

As mentioned before, the routine should give the effect of a continuous flow of movement. Continuity is achieved by a rhythm which allows the routine to flow smoothly from one movement to the next without interruption, although there must be variations in timing in uneven bars exercises. Monotony, of course, must also be avoided. There should be fluency within a single movement, too. It is in achieving this that the knowledge of mechanics is so important.

What are the values of this fluency? First, it has an aesthetic value. An exercise with correct rhythm will be light, graceful, and alive—and consequently, spectacular. The second value of fluency is in economy of effort: the momentum gained in one movement can be utilized in the succeeding one. Therefore, in planning a routine, the direction of movement and body position at the end of a move should determine what the next move should be. The following are examples of good combinations in which one move can facilitate the execution of the succeeding one:

1. Stationary kip (kip from low bar to high bar), cast to flying hip circle.
2. Glide kip catch high bar, straddle over low bar to rear lying position, stationary kip to front support on high bar.
3. Flying hip circle to eagle catch, single-leg shootover to stride position on low bar, mill circle forward.
4. Glide kip on low bar facing high bar, cast to squat on low bar, stand up and jump to front support on high bar, forward hip circle, cast to handstand dismount.

The above examples will now be shown in poor combinations which contain an extra swing:

1. Double-leg bounce off low bar to back pullover high bar, cast (extra swing needed) to flying hip circle.
2. Glide kip catch high bar, straddle over low bar to rear lying position, double-leg bounce off low bar (extra swing needed) to back pullover high bar.
3. Flying hip circle to eagle catch, single-leg shootover to stride position on low bar, mill circle backward (extra swing needed).
4. Glide kip on low bar facing high bar, cast to squat on low bar facing high bar, stand up and jump to front support on high bar, cast (extra swing needed) to handstand dismount.

COACHING HINTS TO INCREASE INDIVIDUAL SCORES

There is no one way to teach or coach. The effectiveness of a method depends to a large extent on the coach and the gymnast. In gymnastics there is little difference between teaching or coaching, since the instruction in both should be individualized. Certainly there are differences in the difficulty level of exercises, in teaching methods, and in the training load. The basic principles of coaching and teaching, however, are the same. Both the teacher and the coach need to know:

1. How to analyze skills.
2. How to condition the gymnast for safe and improved practices.
3. How to present skills in a variety of ways.
4. How to motivate the gymnast.
5. How to meet the particular social and psychological needs of gymnast.

The fundamentals of coaching uneven parallel bars are outlined and explained with examples below. From this outline the teacher can make adjustments to fit her situation:

1. Gymnasts need a technical, analytical approach to the mastering of skills. Knowledge and application of mechanical principles can make crucial differences in success. When the student understands the basic principles of the movements to be mastered, she is ready to analyze the performance of another. This will help her to gain quicker insight into proper form. Teammates, for example, often note things that escape the attention of even the most experienced coach. The writer has used this learning-through-analysis technique with the greatest success in both teaching and coaching situations.
2. The use of visual aids such as films, video tapes, wall charts, and photographs may also help greatly to understand the ideal performance of a skill. A film, for instance, will allow the gymnast to view the movements and analyze them critically. A videotape recorder can be a valuable aid for analyzing one's performance immediately. A routine can be taped in its entirety and instantly shown to the gymnast. The coach can point out the weaknesses in the exercise. When the gymnast has analyzed her work she can repeat her routine immediately and try to correct her mistakes.
3. To aid the gymnast in developing a kinesthetic feeling for the skill, the coach may apply the method known as manipulative teaching. In gymnastics this is called spotting and consists of putting or lifting the performer through the stunt to give her the "feel" of the movement. Thus spotting, besides being a safety device, is also used as an aid in teaching.
4. The use of visual cues is also extremely important in developing the sense of correct body position. For example, in the glide kip the teacher should tell the gymnast to look at her legs as they swing upward until her hips reach the bar level. This will help the gymnast to sense the correct head position and will also eliminate early kipping action.
5. The teacher should help the gymnast to see and feel her movements.

Judging and point deductions should be discussed. Gymnasts should judge each other's performances. This will make them more aware of their own and others' form breaks.

6. It is better to practice two or three moves together than a single movement by itself, unless the movement is exceptionally difficult. The use of short sequences of movement allows the performer to get into and out of a move and so accustoms her to the feeling of continuity required for a fluid routine.

7. Activity on the bars requires strength. The coach should give special exercises for developing strength in the upper arms, shoulders, and abdominal muscles.

8. The gymnast's endurance requirements are peculiar. She needs her strength only for a short time, but to do her short routine without form breaks requires much practice. Endurance in gymnastics can be increased only by practicing the combinations and the routine again and again. Half of the routine should be practiced first and then repeated with another movement added. This pattern should be repeated until the whole routine can be done in good form without stopping. When the entire exercise can be done without too much stress, the gymnast should try to perform it again without resting. Top gymnasts are able to repeat complete routines several times. Only after the exercise has been done in its entirety should the poorly performed skills or combinations be practiced separately.

9. It is suggested that the gymnast use handguards and that the bars be kept clean of chalk by frequent sanding with fine sandpaper, to prevent blisters (which often tear) on the palms of the hands. The gymnast should keep her hands soft with hand lotions. If her hands are sore, it is advisable for the gymnast to refrain from practicing for a day or two.

10. To prepare the gymnasts for competition, a competitive atmosphere should be developed during workouts. Each girl in the group should perform her routine with the teacher as a judge. It is also very helpful for the gymnasts to participate in a demonstration before the meet in order to accustom them to an audience.

11. Mental rehearsal of the routine is very good before competition. The gymnast should think through her entire routine just before her turn. This will give her self-confidence and warm her up for the event.

12. The coach should provide encouragement to her students in the compretition when it is needed. She should make the gymnast realize that the purpose of gymnastics is not to win, but to participate and compete, and that there is no disgrace in losing *if* the gymnast has tried her very best.

EXPANSION OF A BEGINNER'S ROUTINE

Optional routines should be well thought out and planned to demonstrate the gymnast's ability. The gymnast should not immediately work toward a final routine (two superior and four medium difficulties) but rather toward an acceptable composition by starting with a variety of beginning movements. Slowly as her skill develops she may add more and more difficulties and better connecting moves to her routine. She should not completely change her routine but should use some of the same combinations and single movements from her earlier routine so that she will be able to perfect the new routine faster.

In the following examples we can see the development of a student from a beginning to an advanced level.

Beginner Level

(no difficulty in the routine)

Starting position: Stand facing low bar. (Note that the same starting position is used in all the following routines.)

1. Flank vault mount. (Run and take off from two feet from beat board, placing hands in overgrip on low bar. As legs are lifted to right in flank position over low bar, quickly grasp high bar with right hand. End facing high bar in inner rear support position.)
2. Long hang; basket to one leg squat; ¾-turn ending in a rear lying support position, hands on high bar, one foot on bar. (From inner rear support position, hands on high bar. Swing to long hang on high bar. Immediately swing legs in pike position between hands, placing right foot on low bar and extending left leg over low bar. Release high bar with right hand and let body naturally turn to left, ending in one-leg squat on right foot on low bar, with left leg extended inside and holding high bar with left hand. This movement may also be performed in opposite direction. In ¾-turn, swing straight leg under high bar, grasp high bar in crossed mixed grip, and change to overgrip at end of turn.)
3. Single-leg stem rise.
4. Forward roll to double-leg bounce on low bar.
5. From double bounce immediately back hip pullover to high bar.
6. Lower to stride support on low bar.
7. Backward single-knee circle.
8. Knee swing up to catch high bar.
9. Place rear foot on low bar and kick up to back hip pullover to high bar.
10. Modified underswing dismount over low bar. (As body drops back, place one foot on low bar to help to push extended body upward and outward over low bar.)

Low-Intermediate Level
(two medium difficulties)

1. Flank vault mount; grasp high bar in a crossed mixed grip. (If doing the following underswing to left then left hand over right in regular grip and right hand in undergrip.)
2. Underswing half-turn to long hang.
3. Pike at hips on contact with low bar and whip legs backward. Then straddle legs with high lift of hips over low bar to double-leg bounce on low bar.
4. Immediately back hip pullover to high bar.
5. Lower to stride support on low bar.
6. Forward mill circle to catch high bar.
7. Place rear foot on low bar and single-leg stem rise to high bar.
8. Flying hip circle to front support on low bar (accepted as medium difficulty in Age Group USGF and DGWS meets when executed in combination with the preceding and succeeding movement).
9. Single-leg squat-through; half-turn facing high bar. Grasp high bar in overgrip and simultaneously lift straight rear leg over low bar. End in inner rear seat position.
10. Long hang; basket to one-leg squat; ¾-turn ending in rear lying support position, with one foot on low bar.
11. Single-leg stem rise.
12. Underswing dismount over low bar (medium difficulty).

High-Intermediate Level
(six medium difficulties)

1. Squat jump over low bar to catch high bar; underswing half turn to long hang with changing grasp of one hand (medium difficulty).
2. From long hang swing to flying hip circle (medium difficulty).
3. Double-leg squat-through.
4. Forward seat circle to catch high bar (medium difficulty).
5. Stationary kip.
6. Forward hip circle on high bar. (Combination of items 5 and 6 is considered as one medium difficulty.)
7. Flying hip circle to eagle catch (medium difficulty).
8. Single-leg shoot over low bar to stride support on low bar.
9. Forward mill circle to catch high bar.
10. Lift rear leg over low bar to rear lying support position.
11. Stationary kip.

12. Underswing dismount over low bar with half-turn. End facing low bar (medium difficulty).

Advanced Level
(two superior and six medium difficulties)
1. Squat jump over low bar to catch high bar; underswing half turn to long hang with changing grasp of one hand (medium difficulty).
2. From long hang swing to flying hip circle, eagle catch (medium difficulty).
3. Double-leg shoot over low bar to rear support position.
4. Forward seat circle to catch high bar (medium difficulty).
5. Stationary kip.
6. Full twist to catch high bar (superior difficulty).
7. Drop glide kip to double-leg shoot-through (medium difficulty).
8. Backward seat circle (medium difficulty).
9. Seat rise catch high bar. (From rear support on low bar drop body back in pike position and swing under bar half seat circle backward and back up to near-free "V" seat position. Release low bar and catch high bar in regular grip.)
10. Stationary kip.
11. Forward hip circle on high bar. (Combination of items 10 and 11 is considered as one medium difficulty.)
12. Underswing dismount over low bar with full twist (superior difficulty).

We can see in the above routines the gymnast's progression from easy to difficult exercises. The progression is summarized in the following examples:
1. Mount: flank vault mount to squat vault mount.
2. Circling movements: backward single-knee circle to forward mill circle, and then to seat circles.
3. Swinging movements: flying hip circle to front support on low bar to eagle catch.
4. Kipping movements: single-leg stem rise to stationary kip, and then glide kip.
5. Miscellaneous movements: single-leg squat-through to double-leg squat-through.
6. Releases: knee swing up to catch high bar to mill circle forward catch high bar, and then seat circle to catch high bar.
7. Dismounts: modified underswing dismount over low bar to underswing dismount, then underswing dismount with half-turn, and finally underswing dismount over low bar with full turn.

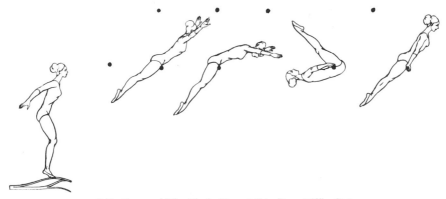

8.7   Forward Hip Circle Mount (Medium Difficulty)

Underview

Overview

8.8   Squat Jump over LB to Catch HB (Medium Difficulty)

**8.9   Glide, Double-Leg Shoot, Straddle Cut, Catch HB Mount
(Medium Difficulty)**

MEDIUM AND SUPERIOR DIFFICULTIES

As previously mentioned, a competition routine should contain four medium and two superior difficulties. The movements and combinations listed below fulfill the requirements for medium and superior difficulty. At the end of the list are illustrations of the lesser-known movements.

In general, a movement with a half-turn is considered of medium difficulty and a movement with a full turn is of superior difficulty.

Medium Difficulties

MOUNTS

Forward hip circle. (See figure 8-7.)

Stand facing low bar, jump squatting legs between hands to rear kip.

Stand back to low bar, jump backward to half-seat circle forward.

Squat jump over low bar to catch high bar, cast half-turn with changing grasp of one hand. (See figure 8-8.)

Straddle jump over low bar to catch high bar in a hang (also with half-turn).

Wolf mount on low bar, half-turn to straddle stand (feet outside hand grasp).

Glide kip; catch high bar. (Note: glide kip to any continuous movement is considered as medium difficulty: for example, glide kip forward hip circle.)

Glide, double-leg shoot, straddle cut, catch high bar. (See figure 8-9.)

CIRCLING MOVEMENTS

Free forward hip circle on low bar to hang on high bar. (See figure 8-10.)

Front support on high bar, cast to straddle stand, forward sole circle to hang.

Flying hip circle, eagle catch.

Forward seat circle.

Backward seat circle on high bar.

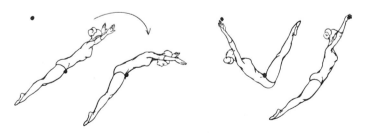

8.10 Forward Hip Circle to Hang on HB (Medium Difficulty)

Knee circle backward.

Knee circle backward to half-turn to front support.

Knee circle backward to catch high bar. (See figure 8-11.)

Sole circles forward or backward (stoop or straddle).

Straddle seat circle forward or backward.

SWINGING MOVEMENTS

From front support on high bar or straddle stand or straddle seat, swing under high bar with half-turn, hip circle on low bar to eagle catch or half-turn to catch high bar in hang.

Half seat circle forward on high bar, dislocate to backward hip circle on low bar to front support. (See figure 8-12.)

Half stoop circle, catch with half-turn high bar, drop to low bar.

8.11   Knee Circle Backward to Catch HB (Medium Difficulty)

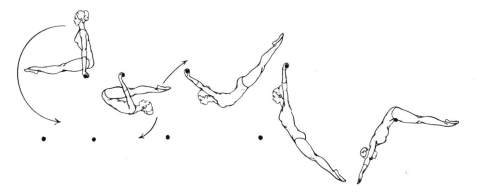

8.12   Half Forward Seat Circle, Dislocate to Backward Hip Circle (Medium Difficulty)

KIPPING MOVEMENTS

Kip on low bar, catch high bar.

Kip to front support to half-turn to rear support.

From hang on high bar facing low bar, kip with legs straddled to front support on high bar.

Shoot through to rear support on high bar from rear lying hang.

Half backward seat circle, disengage legs, kip to front support. (See figure 8-13.)

From rear lying hang, rear kip on high bar. (Note: rear kip from glide during exercise is also considered as medium difficulty.)

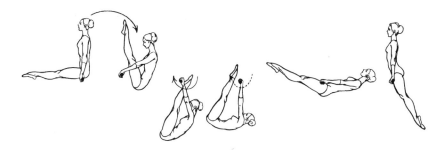

8.13 Half Backward Seat Circle, Disengage Legs, Kip to Front Support (Medium Difficulty)

MISCELLANEOUS MOVEMENTS

Stoop through on high bar.

Straddle jump backward over high bar to hang high bar. (See figure 8-22.)

From front support on high bar, pass legs straddled over bar to rear support.

DISMOUNTS

From high bar back straddle cut off (also with half-turn).

Stoop or straddle jump over both bars.

From front support on high bar underswing dismount over low bar. (See figure 8-14.)

Hecht off the low bar (without twist).

Superior Difficulties
MOUNTS

Jump with full twist to forward hip circle on low bar.

Jump with half-turn to knee circle backward on low bar; catch high bar.

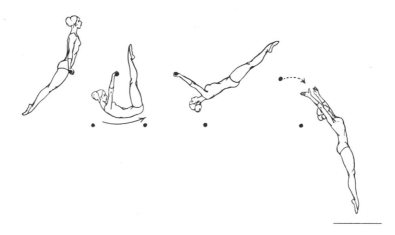

8.14   Underswing Dismount over LB (Medium Difficulty)

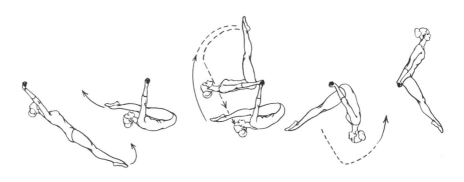

8.15   Rear Kip Mount (Superior Difficulty)

Straddle or squat-jump over low bar, immediate straddle back over low bar
    to glide kip.
Rear kip mount. (See figure 8.15.)
Jump to handstand mount on low bar.

CIRCLING MOVEMENTS

Forward hip circle to handstand on low bar or high bar.
Sole circle backward to handstand.
Free backward hip circle on low bar or high bar to hang.
Flying back hip circle without hands, half-turn to backward knee circle.

Backward hip circle hecht on high bar with half-turn to catch high bar in hang.

Forward seat circle on high bar to straddle cut catch high bar.

Backward seat circle on high bar, facing low bar, to release to front support or to kip on low bar. (See figure 8-16.)

From a rear stand on low bar layout free back fall to catch on low bar into glide kip. (See figure 8-17.)

8.16   Backward Seat Circle on HB, Release to Glide on LB
(Superior Difficulty)

8.17   Layout Free Back Fall to Catch LB, into Glide Kip
(Superior Difficulty)

Seat circle backward on high bar, facing low bar, release high bar, half-turn
knee circle backward without hands.

From front support on low bar, straddle over, knee circle backward without hands.

Backward hip circle on low bar, full turn catch high bar in long hang (catch
in regular or mixed grip).

From front support on high bar, full turn to catch high bar. (See figure 8-18.)

Back uprise, full turn to catch high bar.

Somersault from low bar to catch high bar. (See figure 8-19.)

**8.18   Front Support on HB, Full Turn to Catch HB
(Superior Difficulty)**

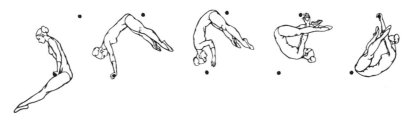

8.19   Somersault from LB to Catch HB (Superior Difficulty)

SWINGING MOVEMENTS

From front support on low bar, facing high bar, or from sole circles, swing
under low bar, catch high bar in piked hang. (See figure 8-20.)

From front support on high bar, facing low bar, or from sole circles, shoot
half-turn out over low bar, glide kip low bar.

8.20   Sole Circle, Catch HB in Piked Hang (Superior Difficulty)

KIPPING MOVEMENTS

Half back seat circle on high bar, back straddle over low bar, glide kip low bar. (As backward momentum stops and forward movement begins from piked position, straddle legs and pass them over low bar by extending hips slightly. Release high bar and catch low bar in hanging position with regular grip.) (Note: any movement from high bar over low bar and catch low bar in hang is of superior difficulty.)

Rear support on high bar, swing under bar (half-seat circle backward) and back up to straddle catch high bar.

Stationary kip to handstand.

Stationary kip free back hip circle to long hang. (Note: free back hip circle following any movement is considered of superior difficulty.)

Stationary kip to straddle on high bar or straddle seat, turn backward, release, catch low bar.

From rear lying hang, rear kip, release, catch low bar to glide kip.

Back uprise. (See figure 8-21.)

Glide, double-leg shoot, straddle cut, catch low bar or high bar. (See figure 8-9.)

8.21   Back Uprise (Superior Difficulty)

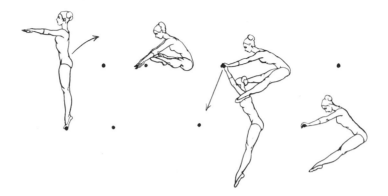

**8.22   Straddle Jump over HB, Catch HB, Drop to LB
(Superior Difficulty)**

**8.23   Handstand Stoop-Through Dismount from HB
(Superior Difficulty)**

MISCELLANEOUS MOVEMENTS

Straddle jump backward over high bar, catch high bar, drop to low bar. (See figure 8-22.)

Straddle jump forward over high bar with half-turn, catch high bar in hang.

Side handstand on high bar, half giant swing to hang.

From handstand on low bar, stoop between hands or straddle to straddle seat support or pass legs under high bar to backward hip circle to front support on low bar.

Side handstand half-turn on low bar.

DISMOUNT

From stand on low bar, kip from neck on high bar with half-turn.

Back straddle cut off over low bar.

Handstand dismounts from high bar (turnover, stoop-through, and straddle-through). (See figure 8-23.)

From front support on high bar, underswing dismount with full turn over low bar.

From front support on high bar, cast somersault forward to front stand. (See figure 8-3.)

From front support on high bar, kip from neck on high bar with full turn.

Hecht off low bar with half or full twist.

Hecht off high bar (either direction).

It should be noted that combining two or more medium difficulties does not result in a superior difficulty.

9
Vaulting

JACQUELYN UPHUES FIE AND KITTY KJELDSEN

GENERAL INTRODUCTION
TO THE CLASSIFICATION OF VAULTS

According to the new DGWS-USGF rules, vaults can be performed in the four following ways: with bent hip, horizontally, diagonally, and vertically. Some vaults lend themselves to more than one manner of execution: for example, the squat vault can be performed in all four ways. The difficulty value of the vault increases as the body straightens and rises higher during the preflight. Other vaults, like the handspring, can be performed only through the vertical position. Twists can be added to the preflight and afterflight of a basic vault for variation and to increase the value of the vault. Thus, a classification of vaults into three major categories with appropriate subcategories appears logical. The basis of this classification is the performance technique:

1. Bent hip
   a. Prolonged hand support vaults
   b. Quick touch vaults
2. Layout
   a. Horizontal vaults
   b. Diagonal vaults
   c. Vertical vaults
3. Twisting
   a. Bent hip twisting vaults
   b. Layout twisting vaults

In general, vaults in the same category have similarities in approach, take-off angle, and other points of execution. However, there are some vaults that seem to defy precise classification. The thief vault, for example, has a one-foot take-off. The headspring places momentary support on the head as well as the hands. The hecht vault has an almost horizontal preflight but a diagonal type afterflight. The yamashita starts out like a vertical vault, but its afterflight takes on several characteristics of the diagonal vaults. These vaults are the exceptional, however, and should be dealt with separately. In the years to come, if the present exploration of gymnastics technique continues, one can foresee the introduction of many other vaults which will defy precise classification.

It should be mentioned here that the FIG, dealing with high-level gymnastics only, has its own classification of vaults. It eliminates all bent hip vaults and combines horizontal and diagonal vaults into one category. The FIG classification is as follows:

1. Horizontal vaults (horizontal and diagonal)
2. Vertical vaults
3. Twisting vaults

The classification given at the beginning of this chapter is clearer than the one offered by FIG. In the English language, the distinction between the terms "horizontal" and "diagonal" is clear. They are two specific terms and we do not have a common word covering both cases, except the term "layout." Taking it a step further and speaking technically, vertical is the ultimate angle of a layout, not a separate classifica-

168

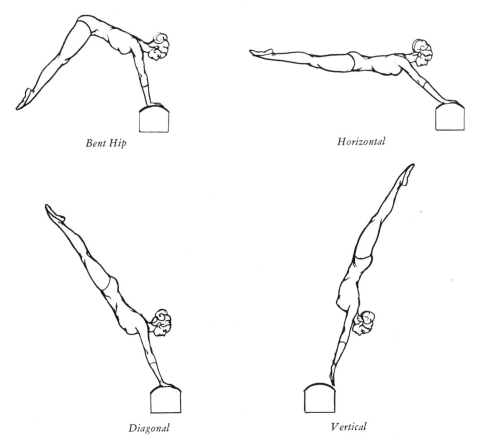

Bent Hip

Horizontal

Diagonal

Vertical

9.1 Four Kinds of Vaults

tion. Therefore, the more detailed classification stated at the beginning of this chapter is clearer in English than the terminology translated from other languages.

TECHNICAL ANALYSIS OF BENT HIP VAULTING

Bent hip vaulting can be classified into two distinct categories:

1. Prolonged hand support vaults (headspring, flank, front, rear, etc.)
2. Quick push vaults (thief, squat, stoop, straddle, etc.)

Prolonged Hand Support Vaults
GENERAL CHARACTERISTICS

Prolonged hand support vaults are generally slower in execution, require less speed, and have a definite stop on the horse. As a result of the lesser speed and stop on the horse, their preflights and afterflights are quite small, as compared to full-speed vaulting. Besides being generally shorter and lower, the preflights and afterflights appear even smaller because of the fact that it is necessary to deviate from the full body layout position in the execution of these phases. Coaches and judges should be fully aware of these characteristics and not expect great flight when teaching or judging prolonged hand support vaults. A well-executed rear vault can earn 5.0 points even though it has relatively little preflight or afterflight. It should not be compared to more advanced vaults in the respect of flight height and length.

Many coaches avoid using prolonged hand support vaults for the reason that they see no carry-over value and are afraid of developing bad habits. While it is true that a great majority of the prolonged hand support vaults are so-called dead-end vaults and not lead-ups to more advanced vaulting, they still serve their purpose in beginning classroom or club work and are used for general training of beginners in Europe and elsewhere.

HEADSPRING (VALUE: 6.0)

The headspring is a unique vault because it calls for a bent arm support and the touching of the horse with one's head. Almost every action considered a "bad habit" in handspring vaults is essential to performance here. Judges may tend to compare the headspring to the handspring, and therefore inexperienced judges tend to ask more from the headspring vault than it is technically capable of providing. By understanding better the techniques necessary to the headspring and accepting the piked preflight, bent arms, slightly whipped afterflight, and other special headspring techniques as normal parts of the vault, the judge and coach can properly reward the girls who are executing it well and stop making comparisons with the handspring, which is really of different character.

The run for the headspring should be of medium length only and not overly vigorous; it is fairly easy to "overrun" this vault, creating an excess of horizontal force which will hinder the actual execution of the vault. The board should be appreciably closer to the horse than for handspring vaults, since a shorter but higher preflight makes the execution of the entire vault livelier and quicker. The take-off is from both feet, following a conventional hurdle. Since the preflight is piked, only a slight blocking action should be used.

In the preflight, the hips keep rising over the head. The arms reach the horse and bend, allowing the top of the head to be placed on the horse. By this time, the hips should be over the head, with the legs approximately horizontal. As soon as the hips have moved beyond the head (the legs are still horizontal), the performer should extend vigorously at the hips, pushing at the same time with her arms and keeping the neck extended. As a result, the center of gravity should move away from the horse in an upward-forward direction. The body should extend in the afterflight, rotating into a vertical position before landing. At the height of the afterflight the head should move forward in order to get in line with the body. The performer should now focus on the wall ahead of her

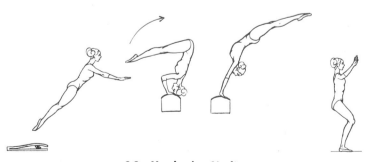

9.2 Headspring Vault

9.3 Flank Vault

in order to regain spatial orientation and land in a balanced position.

Coaches and teachers of this vault should be careful to see that the performer does not extend too early. Her hips should be beyond her head and her position should be slightly off balance in the direction of the flight before the extension occurs.

FLANK VAULT (VALUE: 5.0)

The most important part of the flank vault is the position of complete body extension at the height of the vault while the weight is momentarily resting on one arm. The extension should be sideways to the direction of the vault, and horizontal or above. The flank vault can be executed to the right or the left side, according to the preference of the performer.

The run should be vigorous, with a short high hurdle. A strong block (see figure 9-28) is essential in order to obtain a high angle of take-off; otherwise the horizontal momentum will carry the supporting shoulder in front of the hand, making a good supporting action impossible.

The distance of the board should be approximately one and a half arm lengths from the horse. Take-off follows a conventional hurdle. Both hands are placed on the horse and the hips are raised above the shoulders. Immediately after hand contact, the weight is shifted to the support arm and the other arm is lifted off the horse. The hips are still piked and the legs are still raising sideways away from the support arm. At this point, the performer should be looking at her legs.

The next move is very often omitted, though it is one of the most important moves in the flank vault. As the legs are still rising, the body extends vigorously, so that a full extension is reached at the height of the vault. The head is brought in line with the body. The hips, feet, and free arm move in line with the support arm as the body weight passes over the horse. Just as the legs start to drop, the support arm executes a downward push on the horse, giving vertical direction to the upper body. The body leaves the horse and rotates into a vertical position before landing in a direct line with the center of the horse in a rear stand.

FRONT AND REAR VAULTS (VALUE: 5.0)

Front (also called "face") and rear vaults are, technically speaking, flank vaults with one-fourth turn. In

Front Vault

Rear Vault

9.4   Front and Rear Vault On-Horse Positions

the face vault, the one-fourth turn is executed toward the horse, and in a rear vault, away from the horse. The performer will land with her side to the horse.

Both vaults start out like the flank vault. The distance of the board from the horse and the importance of the block are as for the flank vault. From there, the differences will become apparent. In case of the front vault, both hands contact the horse on the preferred side of the performer, but instead of being parallel to the length of the horse, the hands are parallel to the width of it. The hips rise up in a piked position, and a very slight twist toward the horse is initiated off the board. As the body weight transfers to the hands, the one-fourth twist is completed and body straightens at the hips. At the height of the vault, the body is facing the horse and is at least horizontal, or at a slight upward angle. Momentary support is taken evenly on both arms. As the legs start to fall, the arms execute a downward push on the horse, and the body rotates into a vertical position, before landing crosswise to the horse. The body should NOT pike down, with the hands still resting on the horse. There should be a definite push and a short afterflight.

Another technique for executing the front vault calls for placing the hands on the horse parallel to its length, raising the hips up in a piked position, releasing one arm, extending the body sidewards above

the horizontal, and executing the one-fourth turn toward the support arm. As the legs start to fall, the support arm executes a downward push on the horse, and the body rotates into a vertical position, before landing crosswise to the horse.

The face or front vault becomes more difficult as the angle of the body at the height of the vault rises above horizontal. A vertical face vault is worth 9.7 points. However, in this vault the board is much farther from the horse and the preflight has no pike, which puts the vault into a vertical category. Coaches should be careful that the beginning vaulter does not raise the legs above horizontal by bending the arms and lowering the chest.

In the rear vault, the slight twist away from the horse is initiated off the board. The lead arm contacts the horse first, and then the trail arm. As in the front vault, the hand position is parallel to the width of the horse. Between the two hand contacts, the one-fourth twist is completed. At the top of the vault, the support may momentarily rest on both arms, with the body facing away from the horse in a piked position. The toes are higher than the head, and there is a slight backward lean from the shoulders. As the legs start to drop, the hands exert a vigorous push on the horse and the hips are extended. The body straightens and rotates into a vertical position, landing crosswise to the horse. The hips should not pike down while the hands are still resting on the horse.

Another method for executing the rear vault has both hands contact the horse first, while the body is rising up sideways to the preferred side of the performer. (Refer to the flank vault). At this point, the body weight is transferred to the arm away from the legs, the other arm is released, and the one-fourth turn completed. Now the released arm is placed on the horse and the body support transferred to it. The first support arm is released. The second support arm pushes the body into the afterflight.

Correct face and rear vaults are not easy to execute. Though there is a prolonged hand support on the top of the horse, there is also a definite push into an afterflight, small as it may be, because of the body position and the pushing angle. Most gymnastics textbooks have not analyzed these vaults except in general terms. Consequently, they are often executed in physical education classes with poor technique. As a result the more skilled girls and better coaches shun these vaults as a waste of time. However, if one looks at the European method of executing these vaults, one becomes aware that even prolonged hand support vaults, performed to their maximum, can be challenging, exciting, and worthwhile at the beginning of one's gymnastics career.

Quick Push Vaults
GENERAL CHARACTERISTICS

In quick push vaults, the hands contact the horse ONLY in order to provide additional forward-upward momentum (and sometimes help in change of direction) to the already moving body. The body does not come to rest upon the hands. According to the Newton's Second Law of Motion, the stronger the additional push and the lighter the body to be pushed, the greater the result. In order to take the maximum advantage of this additional push, two factors are necessary:

1. The push must be timed correctly.
2. The push must be rapid.

If the additional push is added to the body while its center of gravity is still moving upward, the forces will work in a linear direction and the result will be much greater. If, on the other hand, the pushing force is exerted while the center of gravity is on its way down, the forces will work in opposition to each other and the effect could be completely nullified.

A pushing action with the shoulder girdle (shrug of the shoulders) is much more rapid, technically superior, and aesthetically more pleasing than any pushing action initiated with bent elbows.

THIEF VAULT (VALUE: 5.0)

Contrary to popular opinion among beginning teachers, the thief vault is not a prolonged hand support vault. The push with hands is used to provide additional forward-upward momentum to the already moving body. The hands do *not* rest on the horse while the legs shoot through and the body arches forward. Here again, seeing Europeans execute thief vaults gives an entirely new view of this skill. The thief vault is unique in that it has a one-foot take-off, and can be likened to a running jump over the horse with the hands coming into play during the second half of the vault. Since FIG rules state that all vaults must be executed by placing the hands on the horse, a thief vault without the use of hands (once a very popular vault with courageous beginners) cannot be used in official competitions.

Since horizontal speed is important in the thief vault, the run should be of medium length and fairly vigorous. The board should be placed a distance of at least half of the girl's body length in front of the horse, so that the forward kick can be executed with a relatively straight leg. The last step before the take-off is executed on the board, with the free leg kicking straight forward-upward. After a strong push off the board, the trail leg joins the lead leg above the horse.

9.5   Thief Vault

By that time, the horizontal speed of the run should have moved the girl over the horse. At this point, the arms come into play, executing a downward-backward push on the horse and enabling the body to gain additional flight. The body straightens during afterflight and rotates into a vertical position for landing.

BENT HIP SQUAT VAULT (VALUE: 5.0)

In many places, as a carry-over from vaulting with the pommeled horse, the squat vault is still taught as a prolonged hand support vault with the body arching off the horse. This technique is not acceptable in artistic gymnastics, or at any level of competition. The squat vault is definitely a quick push vault.

Since flight is important in all quick push vaults, the board should be placed at least half of the body length away from the horse, and the distance increased to one body length or so as the performer becomes more confident of her skill. The run should be quite long and vigorous, with special attention to the blocking action and take-off position (refer to p. oo). Hips are piked right off the board and the knees start moving toward the chest. Upon hand contact, the shoulders should be directly over (not in front of) the hands, with the hips slightly above shoulders and the center of gravity still moving in a forward-upward direction. As a result of the push off the horse, the shoulders should move higher than the hips, and the body should straighten in the afterflight before contacting the ground for landing.

9.6   Bent Hip Squat Vault

9.7 Bent Hip Straddle Vault

BENT HIP STRADDLE VAULT (VALUE: 5.5)

The importance of the run, hurdle, and block and distance of the board are the same as for the squat vault. The hips rise slightly piked off the board, but the legs remain straight and together. Upon hand contact, the hips should be higher than shoulders, with shoulders over the hands and the center of gravity still moving up. During the quick push the legs start to straddle, the shoulders rise above hips, and the body starts to straighten. By the highest point of the after-flight, the legs should be joined together again and the body should be vertical. Coaches should make sure that girls with very flexible hip joints do not execute a side split over the horse. Remember that upon hand contact, the hips should be at least as high as the shoulders.

BENT HIP STOOP VAULT (VALUE: 5.5)

The beginning of the stoop vault is very similar to that of the straddle. Upon the hand contact, the hips should be quite high above the shoulders, with the shoulders still remaining over the hands. As the push is executed and shoulders start to raise, straight legs are brought forward between the hands and the body opens up into a vertical position.

The timing of the stoop vault is very important. If

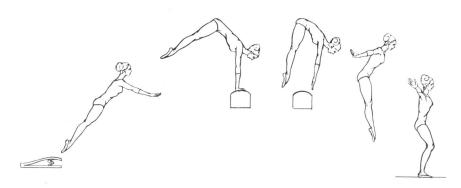

9.8 Bent Hip Stoop Vault

the shoulders are in front of the hands upon hand contact or if the pike is too sharp at that point, it is impossible for the body to open up in the afterflight phase. More important, if the body weight rests on the hands upon the contact (indicating that the center of gravity has stopped rising), the afterflight will be practically non-existent because of the poor body position during the push off from the horse.

Some coaches feel that because of this very critical timing factor, the afterflight in a stoop vault can never be as high or long as in the straddle. The stoop vault has more up-down motion, which cuts into the horizontal velocity and distance of the afterflight.

BENT HIP STRADDLE HALF TWIST (VALUE: 6.0)

Up to the point of pushing off the horse, the straddle half twist is executed just like a regular bent hip straddle vault. During the afterflight, while the body is straightening out of the pike and the legs are joining, the half twist is executed, and the performer lands facing the horse. This twisting action is initiated at the hips and should be completed at the high point of the afterflight.

COMPARATIVE TECHNICAL ANALYSIS OF SELECTED FIG COMPETITIVE VAULTS

Descriptions of ideal technique and hints to spot good movement are presented here to prepare the judge to analyze quickly the several categories in vaulting. She must understand the differences in performance technique that exist between:

1. Horizontal vaults (see figures 9-14 and 9-16).
2. Diagonal layout vaults (see figure 9-15).
3. Vertical vaults (see figure 9-20).
   a. Yamashitas (see figure 9-22).
   b. Twisting vaults (see figures 9-17, 9-18, 9-19, 9-21, and 9-23).

There are two main phases or principal parts in all vaults:

1. First phase: from board until hand contact is made with the horse.
2. Second phase: from hand contact through landing.

These separate phases as they relate to the above-mentioned categories will now be examined.

9.9   Bent Hip Straddle Half-Twist

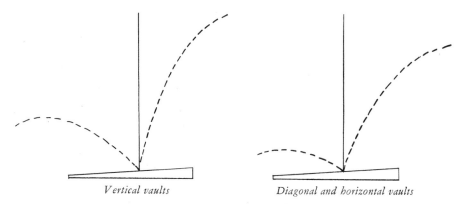

Vertical vaults   *Diagonal and horizontal vaults*

9.10   Hurdle and Take-off

Run and Take-Off

The distance of the board from the horse is optional, depending on the size and strength of the gymnast, but the distance should be greater than the length of the gymnast's body. There must be enough time for proper action during the on-flight before hand contact occurs.

There is no penalty for a poor run, but this will nevertheless affect the entire vault. The essential element is the technique of the run and take-off and not the height or size of the gymnast. (See figure 9-28.)

The contact should occur in the middle of the board toward the forward portion. If the contact is too far forward on the board and the body is inclined forward, the force will be misdirected, resulting in a flat forward flight to the horse. The center of gravity is behind the base of support on initial board contact. The "block" should be executed on the balls of the feet with feet parallel. The body must remain stretched and straight on take-off with the arms reaching toward the vertical. Once the feet leave the board, the center of gravity has moved over the base of support. There is no penalty for a weak or incorrect body position on take-off, but vaulter's technique indicates what can be expected during the on-flight.

The amount of lifting force on the take-off will depend on the speed of the run, the strength of the foot contact and repulsion from the board, and the position of the body in relation to the vertical position of the board. The take-off for vertical vaults will require stronger vertical force than for horizontal and diagonal vaults.

1. In vertical vaults (including twisting and ya-mashita vaults), the body is behind the vertical on board contact and there is a slightly larger step or arc on the hurdle before the board contact. (See figure 9.10.)

2. In diagonal layout and horizontal vaults, the body is closer to the vertical on board contact and is preceded by a lower step or hurdle.

3. In the hecht (horizontal) vault, during the execution the body is nearly vertical and the blocking action on the board is less noticeable. The hurdle is long and low, resembling that for a layout vault.

Preflight

The blocking action on the board must redirect part of the horizontal force (run) into the vertical force, resulting in upward diagonal on-flight. The center of gravity rises and the body begins to rotate. If the body is overarched, there is too much rotation before hand contact with the horse. If piked, there is insufficient rotation, a shortened preflight, and early hand contact. For best results the body must be stretched during the preflight, but not hyperextended or arched.

If the preflight is too high, there will not be enough horizontal speed left to get a good push-off and a resultant good afterflight. The gymnast will "ride" the horse on hands too long and have a flat afterflight.

1. In vertical vaults (including twisting vaults and the yamashita), the body must rise obliquely upward and be high (just above 40°) when hand contact is made. The angle of the body on contact must be greater from the vertical than the angle of body on the pushoff. The arms, shoulders, body, and legs must remain in line until the repulsion occurs. The arm-body angle must be great, but less than 180°, and the angle between the arm and the horse-vertical should be about 120°.

2. During the diagonal layout vaults, the body must rise obliquely forward and be at a 45 degree angle and not more before the hand touch occurs. During horizontal vaults, the body does not rise above the horizontal before hand contact.

3. For both diagonal-layout and horizontal vaults, the arms, shoulders, body, and legs must remain in line until the initial hand touch is made. The straddle, stoop, or squat action does not occur in the preflight phase, but begins upon hand contact with the horse. If the preflight is weak and there is an early hand contact, the legs will bend during the stoop *and* the straddle or the squat action will begin too soon. There will be a poor pushoff and a downward direction to the off-flight. When the straddle movements begin, the body must be piked, but the legs must not come before the shoulders.

4. During the hecht (horizontal) vault, the body retains more forward momentum and exhibits less redirection of horizontal to vertical movement. The desired preflight proceeds in a near-horizontal direction. A true layout position (at 45 degrees) is undesirable; in fact

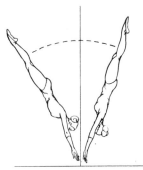 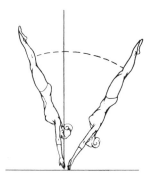 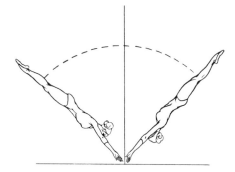

Correct   On-flight angle greater than angle of off-flight.

Incorrect   On-flight angle too narrow; off-flight angle too wide.

Incorrect   Angles too wide.

9.11   Vertical Vaults

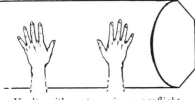

Vaults with no turns in on preflight.

Vaults with quarter-turns in on preflight.

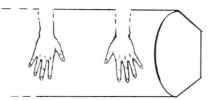

Vaults with half-turns in preflight.

9.12   Hand Placement

the body should be somewhat near the horizontal position. A perfectly stretched body position is not necessary and a slight pike never draws a penalty. Just prior to hand contact, there is a deliberate slight piking of the hips to help the body rise and rotate after the pushoff. The piking action assists the blocking action of the arms on the horse. (See No. 1 in figure 9-16.) Both the pike and the block redirect the horizontal movement to the vertical movement needed during the after-flight stage.

Obviously the preflight phase must be performed with good technique so that the gymnast will have sufficient repulsion. There is little opportunity to actually "style" a vault, since the emphasis is on perfect form and precise technique to attain the desired effect in both on and off phases. Experienced vaulters can vary their arm positions to some extent. The forceful thrust of the arms stretched obliquely upward and outward in a large "V" is definitely spectacular for vertical vaults and may or may not aid the on-flight.

This action positively gives the illusion of a higher and more suspended on-flight.

Arrival on the Horse

The ideal position is with the arms straight and the shoulders in line with the hands (shoulder-width placement of the hands). The hands are in line with the body with fingers always facing forward. The position of the hands in relation to the body is always the same. (See figure 9.12.)

The weight is on the forward part of the hands, not on the heel. The hands completely touch: not just the fingers. The duration of hand contact is very short and the support rolls from the heel of the hand to the fingertips.

1. The push occurs at the peak of the on-flight position (with the center of gravity still moving upward) when the shoulders are able to add to the push through the wrists and fingers.
2. The body should not be moving downward at the time of repulsion.
3. The angle of the body is closer to the vertical now than in the angle of contact.

4. The pushoff functions to bring the body obliquely forward-upward.

Afterflight

The repulsion ability depends greatly on the preflight and angle of arrival on the horse. The reaction time is very short during the pushoff, with no body weight resting on the hands. The body is propelled diagonally upward. The vault is completed at the high point of the afterflight.

1. In all vertical vaults, the arms are straight and there is a stretch from the shoulders with no

accentuation of arch. There is no necessity for strength or special skill to keep straight and right oneself. Both on-flights and off-flights should have about the same height and length, although it is not an error if the afterflight is higher and longer, assuming that the on-flight was not poor. The afterflight of the yamashita varies from that of other vertical vaults in that the arc or trajectory must be higher than the on-flight and the distance is shorter.

2. In horizontal vaults the afterflight is a direct result of the speed of the preflight. When the on-flight is not forceful, the hand contact

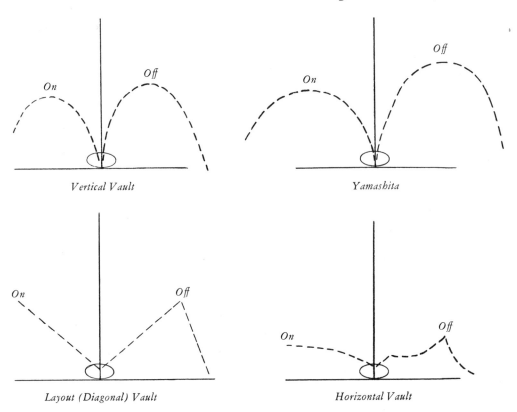

Vertical Vault

Yamashita

Layout (Diagonal) Vault

Horizontal Vault

9.13   Comparison of Preflight and Afterflight Arcs

is early and the body may not clear the horse. The feet may touch, there is prolonged hand support, and the off-flight is too short. It is impossible to straighten the body before landing.

3. In the execution of the diagonal layout and hecht vaults, the opening up of the body depends greatly on what preceded in the first phase. If the first phase is too high, the body moves head first downward with piked body, and no straightening of the body is possible before landing. The repulsion, of course, must be quick and powerful to achieve the desired upward diagonal direction of flight. During the afterflight of the hecht, the body moves forward upward and, as a result of the slight pike and blocking action of the arms, the body motion changes from forward to upward and rotates to a vertical position.

Flight During Turning Vaults

There are three general categories of twisting vaults: those executed with turns in preflight, with turns in afterflight, and with turns in both flights.

The turns in the first phase start from the take-off and the turns in the second phase start from support on the horse. Swiftness of turns is essential. The narrower the angle of pushoff to the vertical, the better the vault. The result is a more precise and quicker turning action during off-flight. The turn in the first phase must be completed before hand contact. In the second phase completion occurs at the height of the off-flight to prepare for the landing. (See figure 9-21. In part 2 of the sequence the turn is complete and in parts 5 and 6 the turn is completed.)

If an on-flight that is too long and low occurs, watch for the body passing around instead of through the vertical position. If the on-flight is too hard and downward into the horse, then the off-flight will also drop off flat.

Landings in General

The exact place on the mat depends on the pushoff, the vault performed, and the size and strength of the gymnast. If the landing is too close to the horse, there was insufficient pushoff. The body must have good afterflight with the proper arc to land in balance. The correct angle of landing is slightly behind the vertical.

In vertical vaults, a low preflight will cause too much body rotation during the afterflight. The result will be several running steps forward, a forward bend in the body and a touch on the mat, or a fall on the knees on landing. If the preflight is too high, the forward momentum is lost, insufficient rotation occurs, and the gymnast will step backward to regain balance and possibly fall on the hips. One step or hop forward is no longer permitted without penalty.

In general, poor landings are caused by poor direction, late pushoff, or insufficient on-flights or off-flights. On mat contact there is a slight forward body bend and a moderate knee bend, and the head remains up.

Balance and Equilibrium in the Overall Vault

The judge must watch the entire vault. The curves on the preflight and the afterflight must be similar, although it is not an error for the second flight to be slightly higher than the first. The shoulders should be in line during the preflight and afterflight. Be sure to watch for body position on diagonal layout vaults in relation to the 45-degree angle and make note if the gymnast straddles, squats, or bends the knees too soon. Pay particular attention to the angles of on-flight and off-flight, the brevity and position of the hand contact, the rapidity and force of the pushoff, and the direction of the afterflight. When evaluating direction, be sure the hands were placed in a straight line with the body and that the landing occurred in line with the vault.

9.14 Horizontal Straddle Vault

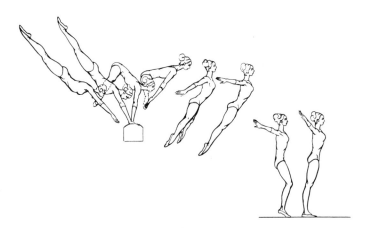

9.15 Diagonal Layout Straddle Vault

9.16 Hecht Vault

9.17 Giant Cartwheel Vault

FIG LIST OF VAULTS FOR COMPETITION

Vaults	Points
1. Straddle vault (horizontal) (figure 9-14)	7.0
2. Layout squat vault (diagonal)	8.5
3. Layout straddle vault (diagonal) (figure 9-15)	9.0
4. Stoop vault (horizontal)	7.0
5. Layout stoop vault (diagonal)	9.0
6. Hecht-swan—arch vault (horizontal) (figure 9-16)	10.0
7. Hecht-swan—arch vault with full twist (horizontal)	10.0
8. High front vault passing through handstand	9.5
9. Giant cartwheel (figure 9-17)	9.8
10. Giant cartwheel—¼ turn out	10.0
11. Handstand—pivot or cartwheel out (figure 9-18)	10.0
12. Giant cartwheel—½ turn out	10.0
13. Giant cartwheel—full turn out	10.0
14. Handstand—¼ turn (figure 9-19)	10.0
15. Handspring (pure vertical) (figure 9-20)	10.0
16. ½ turn into handspring—½ turn out (figure 9-21)	10.0
17. Handspring—full turn out	10.0
18. ½ turn to handstand—full turn off	10.0
19. Yamashita (vertical) (figure 9-22)	10.0
20. Yamashita—½ turn out	10.0
21. Yamashita—full twist out	10.0
22. Giant cartwheel or ¼ turn on—¾ turn off (figure 9-23)	10.0

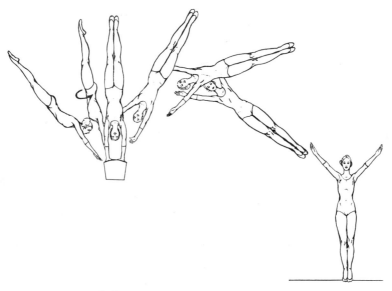

9.18   Handstand Pivot Cartwheel Vault

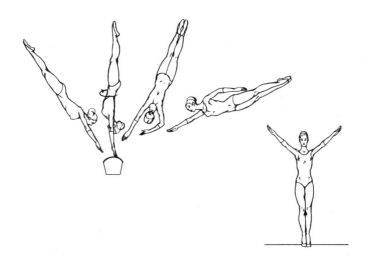

9.19   Handstand Quarter-Turn Vault

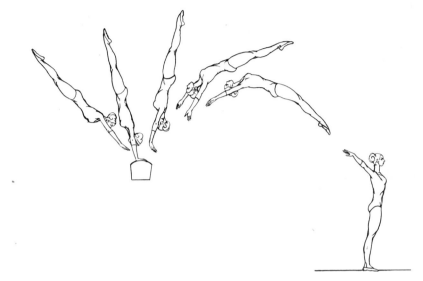

9.20 Handspring Vault

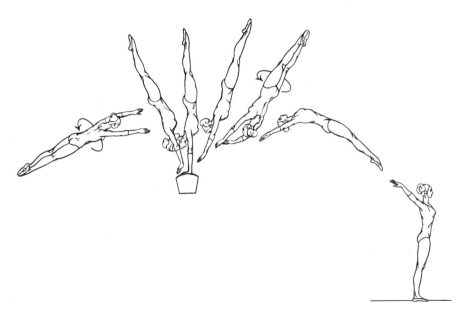

9.21 Half-Turn into Handstand, Half-Turn Out

9.22   Yamashita

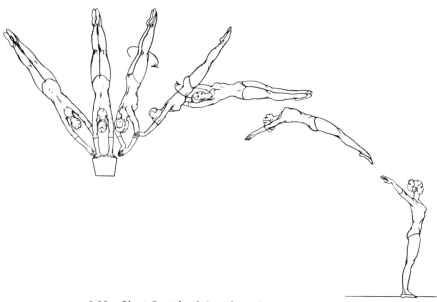

9.23   Giant Cartwheel On, Three-Quarter Turn Off

GUIDE FOR INTERPRETING SPECIFIC PENALTIES AND DEDUCTIONS
General Considerations
The dimensions of the equipment are as follows:

        Horse: Height: 110 cm or 43-5/16"
               Length: 160 cm or 63"
               Width: 40 cm or 15¾"
        Board: Height: 12 cm or 4¾"
               Length: 120 cm or 47¼"
               Width: 60 cm or 23⅝"

All vaults must be performed with both hands placed on top of the horse. The gymnast has the right to two executions each for the optional and compulsory vaults. The best execution of the two vaults is recorded as the official score. Therefore, the gymnast has the right (upon request) to see the score of her first vault before the second attempt is made, since she may wish to vary her second optional performance. This right is not prescribed by rule, but a courtesy followed if time permits.

An additional run is allowed for either one (but not both) of the two vaults, without penalty, provided the gymnast does not come in contact with the horse. If the hands or body contact the horse, the attempt is considered completed. The gymnast may start her run only when the green light is on. She may not run when the red light is on; if she does, the attempt is void.

The coach must stand on the side of the descent, if she must spot. She may not touch the horse, signal or make signs, or speak to the gymnast during performance.

When the gymnast lands, one step in the direction of descent is no longer allowed without drawing a deduction.

The gymnast must announce the *optional* vault to be performed by selecting the corresponding jump number according to the International Table of Vaults and then showing the card to the judges. Calling the vault to the superior judge is sufficient, unless otherwise specified. If the vault selected is not then executed, the vault actually performed will still count, but a 0.5 point deduction will be made.

Judging Qualities
Vaulting is an extremely difficult event to judge. An entire vault is completed within seconds. There must be intense observation of technique followed by rapid recording of penalties. Judges must possess:

    1. The ability for absolute concentration.
    2. Complete understanding of the desired technique for all vaults.
    3. Very good memory.
    4. Alertness.
    5. Trained eyes.

All penalties and deductions must be thoroughly memorized. Once a vault is called, the judge must be able to visualize proper movement and technique and know what faults are likely to occur during execution. Judges must evaluate in general and as a whole the on-flight and off-flight, the pushoff, the direction, the landing, the body position and stretch, and the arc of flights. Then specific penalties are quickly recorded.

Two judges must sit or stand on each side of the horse. Ideally they should be some distance away and on a level lower than the horse looking upward. From this vantage an overall evaluation can be more easily made.

Methods of Judging Compulsory Vaulting

The FIG divides the vault into six categories or phases and establishes guidelines or limits for penalties within each phase. This formula is:

Category	Points
On-flight	2.0
Repulsion, pushoff	2.0
Off-flight	2.0
Position and stretch of body during flight	2.0
Direction of vault	0.5
General balance throughout vault	1.5

Deductions for poor landings are taken from the last two categories, depending on the cause of the poor or unbalanced landing. Stepping to the side, turning on landing 45 or 90 degrees is usually the cause of poor direction, while falling backward or forward or stepping backward or forward is caused by poor balance of flight. Total deductions should for the most part conform to these guidelines.

A list of specific penalties and deductions should be printed for the compulsory vault and sent to all judges and coaches prior to the competition. This will alleviate much discussion and difference of opinion (pertaining to the amount of deductions), especially when lower-level vaults are required. Therefore it is necessary to state the low and high limits for all penalties which may occur.

If the compulsory vault is not performed, a zero is awarded. When the compulsory vault is slightly modified, deductions are made for poor technique. For example, deductions would be made for a poor giant cartwheel vault that looks like a handstand-cartwheel because of improper hand placement and incomplete turn during the preflight.

The superior judge has the power to decide whether a wrong vault was executed and the attempt is void.

Summary of Penalties for Compulsory Vaulting*

1. Application of penalties to compulsory layout vault:
   a. If a horizontal or bent hip vault is executed (which means insufficient elevation or degree of preflight), the vault will *not* be scored zero.
   b. A vault will be penalized according to the specific deductions given in the listing of faults for that specific compulsory vault. (It will not be penalized by 0.5 for performance of the wrong vault.)
   c. Penalties are as follows:
      Layout vault performed at the horizontal .... 2.0 deduction
      Layout vault performed below the horizontal .... 3.5 deduction
   d. The vault *will* be scored zero if an entirely different vault is executed, as in the following examples:
      1. A stoop vault is performed when a form of the straddle or squat is required.

Scratch Area	Value*	Phases	Deductions First Attempt	Deductions Second Attempt
	2.0	Preflight		
	2.0	Repulsion		
	2.0	Afterflight		
	2.0	Stretch of Body		
	.5	Direction		
	1.5	General Balance		
		Neutral Deductions		
		TOTAL DEDUCTIONS		
		FINAL SCORE		

* This column may be eliminated or the values may be placed in parentheses after the respective phase.

9.24   Sample Judge's Worksheet, Compulsory Vaulting

*As approved by the FIG for use in all USA competitions.

    2. A straddle vault is performed when a form of the stoop or squat is required.

    3. A squat vault is performed when a form of the straddle or stoop is required.

2. Application of penalty for insufficient elevation of compulsory horizontal vault:

Horizontal vault performed with bent hips .... 1.5 deduction

3. Application of penalties to compulsory vault executed with higher elevation:

    a. The vault will *not* be scored as zero.

    b. The vault will *not* be credited for the greater preflight.

    c. The vault *will* be penalized by 0.5 (to encourage performance of compulsory vault).

The meet officials must furnish judging work/score sheets outlined according to the FIG formula for efficient scoring and record keeping. (See figure 9-24.)

Method of Judging Optional Vaulting

The FIG divides the vault this time into two phases:

1. First flight. Principle parts are:

    a. Take-off: Position of arms, shoulders, legs; trajectory; lift of body.

    b. Arriving on horse: Position of hands, arms, shoulders, hips, legs.

2. Second flight. Principle parts are:

    a. Repulsion:

        Energy or force of repulsion.

        Vitality of the reaction.

        Balance of the second flight as compared to the first according to the vault executed.

        Stretch and position of the body during the afterflight.

    b. Descent:

        Landing on the floor.

        General direction of the vault.

        General stability of the vault.

This list of phases is rather difficult to work with during competition, since the vault must be instantly analyzed, the specific penalty quickly recorded, and the score rapidly computed. It is much easier to work with fewer categories. Most experienced judges follow one of the following two formulas:

Method 1:

    a. Pre-flight and contact.

    b. Repulsion.

c. Afterflight.

d. General body position and stretch during entire vault.

e. General balance, including direction and landing.

With this method body position and stretch is evaluated in general, placing all deductions for faults in body position into one category.

Method 2:

a. Preflight and contact.

b. Repulsion, afterflight, opening or stretch of the body (horizontal vaults).

c. General balance, including direction and landing.

With this method, all faults and corresponding penalties for body position and stretch are noted during the phase in which the fault occurred.

For example:

1. The penalty for an incomplete turn during preflight is taken from the preflight phase.

2. The penalty for poor stretch and body position at the moment of hand contact is taken during the preflight phase.

VAULTING _____	#1	#2	#2	#1
GYMNAST _____				
Value of Vault	_____	_____	Gymnast #____	Gymnast #____
FIRST PHASE				
Preflight	_____	_____		
Arrival on Horse	_____	_____		
SECOND PHASE			SCORE	SCORE
Repulsion	_____	_____		
Afterflight	_____	_____		
Stretch of Body (Horizontal Vaults)	_____	_____		
THIRD PHASE				
Direction	_____	_____	Signature	Signature
General Balance—Landing	_____	_____		
Spotting—Interference	_____	_____		
TOTAL Deductions	_____	_____		
SCORE	_____	_____		
Judge's Signature				

9.25   Sample Judge's Worksheet, Compulsory and Optional Vaulting

3. The penalty for insufficient stretch during afterflight is taken during the afterflight phase.

4. The penalty for bent arms throughout is taken during the repulsion phase.

All deductions are memorized and, after announcement of the vault, the judge formulates a mental picture of what to expect. She then immediately penalizes those poor techniques with the proper amount, placing the deduction next to the proper phase on her judge's score sheet. It is again the responsibility of the meet officials to supply these score worksheets. The judge's worksheet in figure 9-24 may also be used for optional judging.

Summary of Penalties for Optional Vaulting

The gymnast must announce the optional vault to be performed by selecting the corresponding jump number according to the International Table of Vaults and then showing the card to the judges. Calling the vault to the superior judge is sufficient, unless otherwise specified. If a different vault than the one called is performed, the superior judge will announce the point value on which all judges must base their score.

VAULTS OVER 9.0 POINTS

If the called vault is different from the performed vault, the vault performed is used as the basis for the score. A 0.5 point deduction is taken from the value of the vault performed. Therefore, if a giant cartwheel value at 9.8 is called and the gymnast executes a handstand-pivot cartwheel valued at 10.0, the judges deduct 0.5 from 10.0, leaving 9.5. The judge writes the FIG number of the vault performed and records a −0.5 at the top of her sheet.

VAULTS 9.0 POINTS AND UNDER (STRADDLE, STOOP, SQUAT)

The gymnast calls the vault with the designation of the type of preflight (layout, horizontal, bent hip). The vault executed is scored according to the specific point value of the vault performed. If the judges do not agree as to the degree of elevation, the decision of the superior judge will dictate.

The new point values for vaults 9.0 points and under are as follows:

Vault			Points
Straddle layout 9.0	Horizontal 7.0	Pike 5.5
Stoop layout 9.0	Horizontal 7.0	Pike 5.5
Squat layout 8.5	Horizontal 6.5	Pike 5.0

The judge deducts 0.5 point only if an entirely different vault than the vault called is executed, as in the following examples:

1. For performance of a stoop vault when a form of the straddle or squat is called.
2. For performance of a straddle vault when a form of the stoop or squat is called.
3. For performance of a squat vault when a form of the straddle or stoop is called.

0.5 point is not deducted for performing the vault with a higher elevation than called and the vault is not credited for the greater preflight.

Specific Penalties for Vaults under 10.0 Points

The lower vaults not listed by FIG (Nos. 1 to 9) have been carefully selected and assigned values (recommended by DGWS-USGF) in order to encourage performance and perfection of those vaults requiring techniques and progressions leading up to the 9.0 and 10.0 vaults and to encourage performance in competition of the vault that the gymnast is most capable of executing properly.

LIST OF VAULTS UNDER 10.0 POINTS

Vaults	Rating
1. Rear vault	5.0
2. Front vault	5.0
3. Flank vault	5.0
4. Thief vault	5.0
5. Squat (bent hip)	5.0
6. Stoop (bent hip)	5.5
7. Straddle (bent hip)	5.5
8. Headspring	6.0
9. Squat (horizontal)	6.5
*10. Stoop (horizontal)	7.0
*11. Straddle (horizontal)	7.0
*12. Squat (layout)	8.5
*13. Stoop (layout)	9.0
*14. Straddle (layout)	9.0
*15. High front vault (passing through handstand)	9.5
*16. Handspring	10.0
*17. Giant cartwheel	9.8

Note: If a vault elevated at 7.0 or below is performed with a half-twist during the afterflight, the value will be increased by 0.5 point. (See USGF-DGWS Vaulting Chart, figure 9-26.)

*FIG evaluation in Table of Vaults.

COMMON FAULTS AND PENALTIES

Fault	Penalty
Insufficient preflight between board and horse (vaults 1 to 17)	Up to 1.5
Body bent in preflight (vaults 12 to 17)	Up to 0.5
Body below horizontal when hands contact horse (vaults 12 to 14)	3.5
*Body below horizontal when hands contact horse (vaults 9 to 11)	1.5
*Body at horizontal (vaults 12 to 14)	2.0
Body slightly above horizontal (vaults 12 to 14)	Up to 0.5
Bending legs (vaults 6, 7, 10, 11, 13, 14)	Up to 1.0
Straddling legs too soon (vaults 7, 11, 14)	Up to 0.5
Failure to place hands on top of horse (hands on rear side of horse) (vaults 1 to 17)	Up to 0.5
Failure to lift hips (vault 7) and bring knees to chest (vault 5)	Up to 1.0
Bending arms in support (vaults 1 to 17)	Up to 1.0
Arms completely bent throughout the vault (vaults 15 to 17)	2.5
Failure to extend body completely before landing (vaults 5 to 7, 9 to 14)	Up to 2.0
Touching horse with feet (vaults 1 to 7, 9 to 14)	Up to 0.5
Insufficient pushoff and afterflight (vaults 1 to 4, 8, 15, 16, 17)	1.0 to 2.0
Alternating pushoff hands (vaults 4 to 14, 16)	Up to 0.3
Failure to bring legs together before landing (vaults 7, 11, 14)	Up to 0.3
Failure to lift hips high (vaults 5 to 7)	Up to 1.0
Using strength to get into vertical (vaults 15 to 17)	Up to 1.0
Stop in reversed support at vertical (vaults 15 to 17)	Up to 1.0
Bad direction of vault (vaults 1 to 17)	Up to 0.5
Lack of continuity (vaults with turns) (vaults 1, 2, 15, 17)	Up to 0.5
Failure to lift body to right or left of hand support above the horizontal (vaults 1 to 3)	Up to 1.0
Poor balance of preflight and afterflight patterns (vaults 1 to 4, 8, 15 to 17)	Up to 1.0
Landing on floor heavy and uncertain (vaults 1 to 17)	0.2
Landing out of balance (vaults 1 to 17)	Up to 0.3
Touching hands to floor (vaults 1 to 17)	0.5
Support of hands on floor (vaults 1 to 17)	1.0
Landing on knees (vaults 1 to 17)	1.5
Landing with support of body against horse (vaults 1 to 17)	1.5
Coach between horse and board (vaults 1 to 17)	1.0

*For all competitions in the U.S.A.

Landing on seat (vaults 1 to 17) 2.0
Aid of coach in landing (vaults 1 to 17) 2.0

The vault receives a zero rating if it is assisted by the coach during the vault, or if it is interrupted by feet resting or by a seated position on the horse.

Penalties for faulty landings will be the same for all vaults rated from 5.0 to 10.0 points.

In order to compute the deduction systematically and quickly, a judge must be familiar with the 10.0 point vault and definitely know how much can be deducted for a specific fault: for example up to 1.5 in the preflight phase. She must also be aware, for example, that during the execution of a horizontal straddle vault, the full deduction for preflight cannot be 1.5, since this vault is worth only 7.0 and also does not require for good performance the same amount of preflight as a 9.0 or 10.0 point vault. Deductions for faults become less severe as the value of the vault diminshes. Therefore, the practice of tempering or adjusting the amount of a penalty is applied to vaults rated below 10.0 points.

Those vaults rated at 5.0 (rear, front, flank, thief, and squat) may easily be judged according to this suggested evaluation of phases:

1.0 Preflight.
1.0 Repulsion.
1.0 Afterflight.
1.0 Body position during entire vault.
1.0 General balance, direction, landing.

Vault Performed	Value
1. Flank	5.0
2. Front	5.0
3. Rear	5.0
4. Thief	5.0
5. Headspring	6.0
6. Squat—bent hip ascent	5.0
7. Squat—horizontal	6.5
8. Squat—layout	8.5
9. Stoop—bent hip ascent	5.5
10. Stoop—horizontal	7.0
11. Stoop—layout	9.0
12. Straddle—bent hip ascent	5.5
13. Straddle—horizontal	7.0
14. Straddle—layout	9.0

Any vault evaluated at 7.0 points or below that is performed with a half-twist increases its value by an additional 0.5 point.

An additional 0.5 point penalty is taken from the value of the vault "called" when a different vault is performed.

9.26 Lower Level Vaults as Recommended by USGF-DGWS

SPECIFIC PENALTIES FOR VAULTS LISTED IN FIG TABLE

The penalties listed below are categorized according to:

1. Type of vault (vertical, Yamashita, horizontal, hecht, vertical with turn).
2. Phase in which the fault occurs (first phase: until hand contact is made; second phase: from repulsion to landing).

Preflight to On-Horse Contact

Vertical Vaults and Yamashita   Penalty

Insufficient flight	Up to 1.5
Body bent during flight	Up to 0.5
Body bent before inverted support	Up to 1.0
Using force to establish support	Up to 1.0
Arms slightly bent at support	0.3 to 0.5
Arms completely flexed (bent to any degree throughout)	2.5
Stopping in inverted support	0.3 to 0.5
Omission of passing through vertical	1.0
Arms, shoulders, body not in straight line	0.5
During flight, legs bent	Up to 0.5
During flight, legs apart	Up to 0.5
Shoulders forward at inverted support (in extreme cases the penalty is 1.0, the same as not passing through the vertical)	Up to 1.0

Horizontal Vaults (Layout)

Body below horizontal	3.5
Body just horizontal	2.0
Body slightly above horizontal	0.5

Turning Vaults

Turn in first flight not complete before hand contact	0.5

Afterflight

Vertical Vaults and Yamashita

No afterflight, insufficient repulsion	1.0 to 2.0
Late removal of hands	0.3 to 0.5
Alternate repulsion	Up to 0.3
Arms, shoulders, body not in line	Up to 0.5
Bad direction, crooked vault	Up to 0.5
Poor balance of preflight and afterflight phases	Up to 1.0

Horizontal Vaults

Straddling or tucking too soon	Up to 0.5
Bending legs in stoop vault	Up to 1.0
Omission of stretch of body in second flight	2.0
Late opening of body before landing	0.3 to 0.5

Touching horse with feet .... Up to 0.5

Bad direction, crooked vault .... Up to 0.5

Late removal of hands .... 0.3 to 0.5

Turning Vaults

Incomplete turns (turn not completed before landing) 0.5

Bad direction 0.5

Failing to pass through the vertical .... Up to 1.0

Arms, shoulders, and body not in line .... Up to 0.5

Lack of continuity .... Up to 0.5

Late repulsion of hands .... Up to 0.5

Poor balance of preflight and afterflight phases .... Up to 1.0

Yamashita Vault

Afterflight does not rise (hips must rise) 0.5

Insufficient opening up in afterflight .... Up to 2.0

Hecht Vault

Bending legs .... Up to 1.0

Insufficient opening up (rising up) in afterflight .... Up to 2.0

Landings

Arriving on floor heavy and uncertain 0.2

Arriving on floor out of balance .... Up to 0.3

Touching hands on floor 0.5

Supporting hands on floor 1.0

Falling on knees 1.5

Falling on hips 2.0

Falling against horse 1.5

Coaching

Coach between board and horse 1.0

Coach making signs to gymnast 0.3

Assisting on vault .... Vault void

Assisting on landing 2.0

Coach touching horse 0.2

Undisciplined conduct of gymnast 0.2

Total lack of discipline of gymnast (giving up without any
effort) .... Vault void

COACHING HINTS FOR VAULTING

Vaulting is one of the least understood of the girls' events. The entire event consists of only one main movement: the vault over the horse. For maximum execution
of this move, everything must be close to perfection, including the preparation of

the run, the run itself, hurdle, take-off position, and other phases that follow. Nothing can be covered up or pulled through by compensating somewhere else. Therefore, understanding of all the mechanical principles and coaching techniques involved is very important to every judge, coach, and gymnast.

Conditioning for Vaulting

Conditioning for vaulting is very often overlooked since the event is of such short duration. Yet, the legs, ankles, and shoulders have a short and intense strain put upon them during the vault and they must be prepared to take it. The following conditioning measures are suggested.

1. Time the girls in 50 yard dashes, urging them to run as fast as they can. For better carryover to vaulting, have the girls use a standing start rather than a crouched start.
2. For quick ankle action, have the girls jump rope. This is also an excellent way to build up endurance for other events.
3. Practice "double touch" handstands on the floor. Have a girl kick into the handstand position (someone can catch her legs at the top since balance is not of essence here) and as the body weight transfers over her hands, have her hop forward on both hands using only a shoulder push for power.
4. Use trampoline work to develop the kinesthetic sense and knowledge of different body positions in the air.
5. Practice tumbling to develop quick "punching" action with the legs as well as a good sense of body positions. The good tumbler will usually also make a good vaulter.

Run and Approach

The vaulter has to be able to run. The type of running employed should be close to sprint style. Many girls run on their heels or use an extremely poor arm motion. If necessary, turn to the track coach at the high school or college for help in analyzing the performer's running style. A few general hints for the beginner are given below.

Run on the toes with the body leaning slightly forward. Lift up the knees in front. The arms should be slightly bent at the elbows, swinging forward and back parallel to the body, not crosswise or on a diagonal. The length of the run is optional, but at the end of the run the vaulter should be moving at, or close to, her maximum velocity. A vaulter should watch the board during her approach. Her run may vary slightly from trial to trial, but watching the board gives a chance to make small adjustments along the way. If the adjustments are major, the starting point of the run might have to be changed. A good vaulter should be able to de-

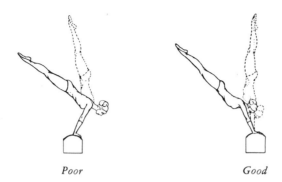

Poor   *Good*

9.27 Shoulder-Hand Relationship upon Contacting Horse

Poor Position Shoulders are in front of hands; the vaulter falls into the after-flight.

Good Position Shoulders are over (or behind) hands; the vaulter is able to push and rise in the afterflight.

pend on the consistency of her run and concentrate on the execution of the vault. During the last step before the hurdle, eyes should be shifted from the board to the horse. The distance of the board from the horse should depend upon the vault to be performed and the natural speed of the girl.

In general, lower level vaults, and, specifically, prolonged hand support vaults, require a fairly close board placement.

In layout and vertical vaulting, placement of the board too close will usually result in a piked preflight and a slower vault resulting from insufficient speed, since the vaulter is afraid to run into the horse.

Moving the board back from the horse does not automatically make the vault better. The distance of the board from the horse does NOT necessarily signify a good vault. If the board is moved back, the vaulter has to compensate by running faster and by blocking more upon take-off. (See figure 9-29.) If the vaulter does not run faster, she will tend to lean forward upon take-off from the board in order to make sure that she gets to the horse. This will result in a long and flat preflight, and she may stall on top of the horse, causing a noticeable lack of afterflight.

If the vaulter increases the speed of her run but does not block more upon take-off, she will again have a long, flat preflight. In addition, her shoulders will be in front of her hands upon contact with the horse. It is impossible to exert any push with the shoulders in this position. The result will be a fast, low afterflight directed downward, with no straightening of the body.

Lower level vaults can be overpowered by a long and fast run. Advanced vaults, however, should use a fairly long run, precisely determined so that the starting point is always the same. A long but slow run is only a waste of energy. The vaulter should start slow, accelerating as she approaches the board. Two-thirds of the way through the run the vaulter should be going at her maximum speed, maintaining it through the hurdle. If a vaulter accelerates too fast, she will probably be slowing down by the time she gets to the board. Acceleration should be gradual at first, with the maximum speed reached about twenty feet in front of the board.

A vaulter should know the exact distance of the board from the horse for each vault she is going to execute. She should also know the exact distance of the starting point of her run from the board (or the horse). Some vaulters like to mark the approximate point at which they start their hurdle. A vaulter who only guesses these distances is never sure that she will hit the board with the correct foot for her take-off. Adjusting the steps along the way will only reduce the increase in speed and cause uncertainty in the vault.

Another important visual cue is the focus of the eyes during the run. At the beginning of the run, the vaulter should look at the board. When she begins the hurdle she should lift her eyes to the horse. Looking at the board after the hurdle begins puts the head and body into a poor position for the take-off. Looking at the horse during the run will, on the other hand, hinder the vaulter in making small adjustments in her steps and being sure of her take-off position.

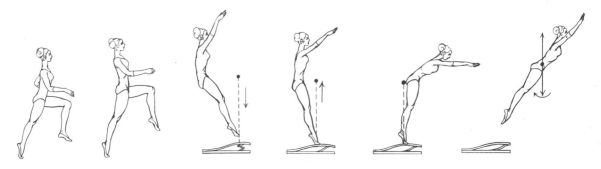

9.28   Run, Hurdle, Blocking Action, and Take-off Positions in Vaulting

Run   Lean forward slightly.

Last Step   Lean back, knee up.

Hurdle and Block   Reach out with feet.

Take-off   Body straight, back slightly rounded, no forward lean.

Wrong Take-off   Too much forward lean.

First Part of Preflight   Straight body rotating around the center of gravity.

Hurdle

The last running step should be taken on the floor in front of the board. The back leg is brought forward and the vaulter lands with both feet on the board at the same time. This is called the hurdle. The hurdle should be low and relatively long, not short and high like a jump off a diving board. The Reuther board used for vaulting has very little "give." Therefore, the take-off should be initiated with a quick ankle action upon contacting the board.

Hurdles for low level vaulting are, generally speaking, relatively short and high. As the distance and speed of the run increase, the hurdles should become longer and lower. Vertical vaults need somewhat shorter and higher hurdles than diagonal vaults, but all hurdles in advanced vaulting should be, generally speaking, long and low. In order to put her body into the best position for the hurdle and facilitate a good blocking action, a vaulter should:

1. Lean back during the *last step* preceding the hurdle (*not* before).
2. Lift the back knee forward and upward into the hurdle.
3. Raise her focal point from the board to the horse during the hurdle.
4. Start raising her arms up over the head.

Blocking Action

Newton's First Law of Motion states that a body in motion will stay in motion until acted upon by an outside force. This description fits a running gymnast. She is in forward motion and will keep moving in that direction until she herself helps to redirect some of this motion, so that her body will rise and go over the horse. The hurdle and the "block" are used to add momentum to the gymnast and to redirect part of her forward movement into upward movement.

During the run the girl's center of gravity is in front of her feet. If she makes no effort to change this, her center of gravity will be so far ahead of her toes that she will take off from the board with a definite forward lean and the momentum will tend to carry her right into the horse. In an effort to avoid this, a beginner is apt to slow down her run, and as a result the entire vault will suffer.

In order to redirect the center of gravity, the "block" comes into use. After the last step and while executing the hurdle, the performer should reach forward with both legs and contact the board with her center of gravity BEHIND the balls of her feet. Now, by the time she pushes off the board, her center of gravity will have traveled over her toes, and will not be in front of her toes. As a result, she will leave the board with the center of gravity traveling in a much higher diagonal path and she will achieve a good, high preflight before getting on the horse.

A quick review: the vaulter should lean back slightly as the knee is brought forward into the hurdle, reach forward with both feet to contact the board with the toes ahead of the center of gravity, and push off with a quick ankle action. This

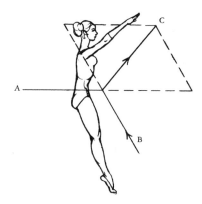

9.29 Blocking in Vaulting

A. Direction of the run.

B. Reaction from the push with legs.

C. Direction of rise of the center of gravity.

happens so fast that there is no time to think about all these cues while performing the hurdle. They should be concentrated upon one at a time, using a simple vault, until the whole approach becomes almost automatic.

The Take-Off

The take-off should be executed off the balls of the feet, utilizing a quick ankle action. The feet should contact the board ahead of the center of gravity. There should be no sharp bend at the hip joint: just a gentle rounding of the upper back. The arms should be moving to an overhead position.

There are several theories about the best arm action during the hurdle and take-off. Is it best to reach forward-upward as in the action of springboard diving, or to move the arms sideward to an overhead position during the hurdle? Analyzing movies of the Olympic vaulters shows that even they use a variety of arm styles.

The purpose of the arm action is to give additional lift to the body and to assist in gaining the proper direction in preflight. Most vaulters raise the arms to just above head height, or, to be more specific, the elbows are thrust up to approximately forehead height. This action, coordinated with the angle of take-off, should result in a desired direction of the preflight.

At this point in the arm lift, the upward thrust is decelerated, resulting in a lightening of the body weight (also referred to as the "elevator principle"*). This

*Stanley Plagenhoeff, "Patterns of Human Motion," Englewood Cliffs, N. J.: Prentice-Hall, 1971.

lightening of the body results in a greater flight, provided the angle and *power* of take-off remain constant.

The take-off *position,* however, must be precise. (See figure 9-28.) It should be understood and practiced until it becomes a habit. The biggest mistake upon take-off is leaning toward the horse. Even after executing the hurdle correctly, many girls tend to lean forward with their upper body by bending at the hips at the moment they leave the board. A good hurdle and block become almost useless if they are counteracted in this manner. In order for the center of gravity to be over the balls of the feet during take-off, the body and legs should be vertical and relatively straight, with the arms reaching forward-upward in front of the face.

Preflight

Once she has taken off from the board, the vaulter has little control over the height or length of her preflight. The preflight is a result of the speed of the run, the blocking action, and the take-off position. Any mistakes in the take-off position are clearly reflected in the preflight, as the following cause and effect listing shows: For example:

Action	*Result*
The vaulter leans forward off the board, bending at the hips.	1. Long, flat preflight.
	2. Hitting the horse too hard.
	3. Riding the horse on the way up.
	4. Bent elbows in inverted support.
The vaulter arches her lower back upon take-off, placing the center of gravity in front of her toes (also called arching off the board or lifting the heels into the vault).	1. The vaulter rotates right over the board. From there on, her preflight has a downward direction.
	2. Low, arched body position in the preflight.
	3. Sagging at the waist upon contact with the horse.
	4. Prolonged hand contact with the horse.

Push-Off

The push-off should occur immediately upon hand contact and should use a shrugging action of the shoulders. If all previous phases of the vault have been properly executed, the vaulter should have little trouble pushing off at the correct angle. The push-off angle should be small, and the direction as close to vertical as possible.

However, if the previous phases have been improperly executed, the vaulter's body position could make it physically impossible for her to exert any push at all. Coaches should recognize that the lack of push-off is, in most cases, caused by mistakes in the first phase of the vault. Unless these mistakes are corrected, very little progress can be made toward rapidity and strength in the push. For maximum results, the push should occur while the center of gravity is at the peak of its curve, NOT on the way down.

Afterflight

As in the preflight, the correctness of the previous phases of the vault determines the quality of the afterflight. For example, a vaulter should open up in the after-flight of bent hip and diagonal vaults, but this is possible only if the push off the horse can be exerted at the correct angle. Only if the reaction from the push moves the vaulter's shoulders in a forward-upward direction, is she able to open up as prescribed by the rules. The correct angle of the push is determined by the shoulder-arm relationship upon hand contact with the horse, which in turn is the result of the take-off angle and preflight. (See figure 9-27.)

Afterflight for inverted vaults should rise off the horse, describing a graceful arc before landing. This arc should be similar to the arc described by the body in the preflight. The head should stay between the arms and in line with the body until the height of the afterflight has been reached. From that point, the head comes slightly forward and the eyes focus high on the wall in front of the vaulter in order to place the body in a good landing position. (One of the most common mistakes is leaving the head back throughout the afterflight.)

In vaults requiring twisting in the afterflight, the twist is initiated off the horse but should be completed during the first phase of the afterflight. The arms during the twist should remain in an overhead position, with the body twisting along the long axis. Coaches should make sure that the vaulter does not rest on the horse with one hand while twisting, and then push into the afterflight.

Landing

A relatively soft and controlled landing is the result of a good afterflight. If the push off the horse is performed at the correct angle and the body is able to open up, a good landing should be no problem. An uncontrolled vault will also have an uncontrolled landing.

Research has shown that it is best not to go into deep knee bends after landing from heights. The vaulter should resist the downward pull of the landing by going only into a small knee bend, with her hips behind the balls of the feet and the shoulders over the hips. Arms should be diagonally up and the head in line with the body. There should be no need for additional steps or shifts in weight.

Visual Cues During Preflight, Push Off the Horse, Afterflight, and Landing

Visual cues during these phases of the vault are very important, since they help in maintaining correct body position and regaining equilibrium at the end of the vault. During the run, the gymnast watches the board. In the hurdle she focuses on the horse. During the preflight, the eyes should still focus on the horse. It is especially important in diagonal and vertical vaults that the head is not tucked *before* the hands contact the horse. Tucking the head too early will give the body additional rotation, which shortens the preflight. The vaulter will land with her hands on the close side instead of the top of the horse, resulting in early rotation over the horse and a complete lack of afterflight.

In all vaults, the vaulter should look at her hands on the horse until they push off. During the first part of the afterflight, the head stays back. As the top of the afterflight is reached, the head comes forward into alignment with the body, with the eyes focusing on the wall ahead of the vaulter. This focus will help the vaulter to regain spatial orientation and facilitate a steadier landing. Bringing the head forward too early in the afterflight flattens the arc of the flight. Leaving the head back too long makes it impossible to straighten the body in the afterflight and land in a correct position.

In diagonal vaults, the focus is shifted from the horse to the mat in front of the horse during the push-off. During the afterflight the eyes seek out a point on the wall ahead of the vaulter or a point on the floor well in front of the landing.

In bent hip vaulting, the focus during afterflight and landing depends on the body positions during these phases of the vault. The head should remain in line with the body and the eyes should seek a focal point for better control during the landing.

General Coaching Hints

The vaulting coach must know the mechanics and the cause-effect relationship of the run, hurdle, block, take-off position, and landing, as they apply to all types of vaults.

In addition, here are some general hints:

1. Do not neglect the conditioning of legs, ankles, and shoulders.
2. When teaching new vaults, put the gymnast through the landing position first. She will then be less apprehensive about the second half of the vault and will concentrate on the most important elements in the first half. For example, when starting to teach a handspring, have the vaulters cartwheel to a handstand on the horse and push into an afterflight (with spotting). Then add the run and the straight body take-off, using spotters on both sides of the horse, if necessary. With fears of the

unknown eliminated, the gymnast will concentrate on "feeling" the body positions of the vault.

3. If possible, minimize the shock of landing by the use of crash pads or thickly padded landing surfaces during the learning stages of the vault.

4. Keep vaulting practices short but vigorous. Be especially aware of girls who tend to develop shin splints easily.

5. At the beginning of the season practice only the correct running, blocking, and take-off positions, using vaults that are familiar to the gymnasts. When these phases are mechanically correct new vaults may be introduced. The results will be worth the effort. Do not build on poor foundations: the gymnast should have a good horizontal vault before a layout is introduced, or a good and dependable handstand before any twists are added.

6. Be careful not to overemphasize the preflight of the vault. The preflight is, after all, only one phase of the vault. Good afterflight and landing are essential for high scores.

It is possible to have the preflight too long or too high. Here are the common consequences:

Action	Result
Preflight too long and probably too flat.	The board is too far out for the speed and skill of the gymnast. She leans forward off the board. As a result, she will have either prolonged hand support on the horse or hit the horse with her shoulders in front of her hands, being unable to push into a high afterflight.
Preflight too high.	The girl arches off the board. Her hips are in front of her toes while pushing off. She rotates too early and lands on the horse in an almost vertical position. The results are: 1. Bent elbows upon contact, because the vaulter is coming straight down. 2. Prolonged hand contact with the horse while the hips ride into an off-balanced position.

3. Weak push into the afterflight, because the vaulter is starting from a "dead" position.
4. Short, low afterflight because of the weak push.
5. Bent-arm push-off, since a shoulder shrug is almost impossible from that position.

Preflight too long and too high.

The girl "stalls out" when she reaches the horse. She has no more horizontal speed left. As a result, the push into the afterflight will either be muscled (bent elbows) or non-existent. The gymnast falls or arches off the horse, after executing a spectacular preflight.

Shin Splints

Shin splints have a way of appearing when least expected. Some gymnasts seem much more susceptible to them than others. They can be quite incapacitating and, according to some medical authorities, can have some harmful long-run effects.

Medical authorities disagree about the exact nature and relief of shin splints. The only agreement is that there is no cure. Relief can be obtained only by eliminating the cause, which seems to be landing or running on relatively hard surfaces.

Many coaches, trainers and athletes have developed their own different ways of dealing with the problem of shin splints. Some like to tape the shins, others support the arches by taping, and still others prefer the wearing of thick-soled shoes or sneakers. Wearing knee socks during practice seems to help some.

Preventatives such as landing in a crash pad, padding the runway and even the take-off board with mats, taping shins or arches before the onset of shin splints, wearing sneakers and knee socks while practicing, along with carefully spacing practices, can delay the onset of shin splints and get a susceptible team safely through the season. However, once the shin splints are there, rest seems to be the only cure.

10

Psychology of Coaching

KITTY KJELDSEN

A specialized psychology of coaching is a totally new concept to most women physical educators or lay coaches. Some do not understand it, and others reject the idea that coaching should be in any way different from teaching an advanced class. Very few colleges and universities offer coaching courses for women, and even fewer have offerings in the psychology of coaching.

According to Patsy Neal in *Coaching Methods for Women*,[1] (one of the very few books available in this field), coaching is both an art and a science. Very few women are instinctive coaches; they often lack highly skilled and organized athletic experiences in their own backgrounds. A great number of women coaches are doing the job not because they are prepared for it, but because they either are interested in providing competitive experiences for girls or happened to be handy when a coach was needed for a particular sport.

In view of these circumstances, it becomes doubly important in examining the coach's role to draw from the disciplines of psychology and sociology. No coach-competitor relationship can be complete without understanding the basic psychological makeup of the personalities involved and the implications of a given social environment.

Dr. Bruce Ogilvie, in *Problem Athletes and How*

to Handle Them,[2] feels that a successful program or technique to modify the behavior of athletes must take into account the personality of the coach. Every human has his own personal "blind spots." The best protection against limiting one's effectiveness by such unconscious mechanisms is to examine one's motives for being a coach.

Observation of coaches during practices and competitions often reveals two distinct personality types. At one extreme is the completely autocratic coach. To her (or him), there is only one way to do things: the coach's way. From the simplest warm-ups to finished routines, every action of the gymnasts tends to bear the distinctive stamp of the personality and beliefs of the coach. Her students become dependent on her guidance and judgment to the point of lacking opinions of their own. Very often the autocratic coach is also a limelight stealer. During practices or competitions, she is the only person allowed to spot a performer. Girls are unable to perform their routines without the presence of the coach, since they do not trust anyone else for spotting or movement analysis. During a meet this coach often makes a big display of checking and rechecking the apparatus before every performance and insists upon standing by the apparatus even if there is no critical spotting to be done.

1. Reading, Massachusetts: Addison-Wesley, 1969.

2. Bruce Ogilvie and Thomas Tutko, *Problem Athletes and How to Handle Them* (Los Altos, California: TAF news, 1966).

At the end of the routine, the coach is there to share the limelight with the gymnast and often whisks her away from well-deserved applause with an obvious display of overprotectiveness or a lecture on what to do differently the next time.

The autocratic coach is often satisfying her own needs for ego involvement by coaching a team. She wants to show how successful *her* work has been or, in case of an exceptionally talented student, what *she* has produced. In the great majority of cases, this coach has not been a successful performer herself and coaching is her way of getting to be known in the field.

At the other end of the scale is the timid coach who is new in the game and afraid to start. She lacks confidence in her own ability to spot or coach students and is afraid to display her lack of knowledge in front of the team. Often the timid coach tries to avoid direct coaching or spotting situations herself by encouraging the students to work with each other or to try things out by trial and error. She is reluctant to offer advice or criticism and ends up by being just another body in the gymnasium. Under the guise of promoting independence, she turns the whole team over to the team members and very seldom intervenes. In the final analysis, she ends up being a little more than a chaperone or adult manager traveling with the team.

The timid coach, in many cases, does not want the job in the first place. She may have had some experience with the sport, but has discovered very quickly that the level of competitive gymnastics in this particular area is beyond her. Her team ends up being a hodge-podge of individuals who have to learn from each other and can go only as far as they can take themselves.

Most coaches, after a thorough self-examination, will admit that they fall somewhere between the two extremes. Success in participation itself does not guarantee that a person will make a good coach. There are many other factors involved.

Being an understanding and mature coach is not easy for most people. It demands certain personality traits which some have by nature but which many must work constantly to develop. The mature coach either knows her area well or is not ashamed to admit her weaknesses and learn along with her girls in order to be better prepared in the future. A talented student and her novice coach can greatly assist each other in this phase of development if both are mature enough to understand the situation. The emotionally well-adjusted coach realizes that there can be several ways to accomplish one's goals. She keeps up with the latest medical and scientific advances in the fields related to training and gymnastics (e.g., weight control, conditioning with different methods, prevention of certain injuries, etc.) and sets realistic goals for the team. The entire team is invited to share in this process and discuss all aspects of it, but once the final decisions are made, jointly or otherwise, it is up to the coach to see that the decisions are observed by every team member.

A mature coach does not need to put herself into the limelight during performances or meet situations. If her team has been well trained, she can, relatively speaking, sit back and *try* to relax. The coach should be more than willing to assist her girls whenever it is needed but should stay out of the limelight. The outcome of the competition is in the hands of the competitors. A coach cannot physically win a meet for them. Her role should be to offer encouragement and moral support from behind the lines and to be physically present when that is necessary for the best and safest performance of a competitor. The focus, however, should be on her competitors and not on the coach.

On the other hand, a coach should instill in her girls the desire to win and the confidence that they can do so, unless the opponent is clearly superior, in which case the girls should be encouraged to go for the best individual score. A coach who is indifferent to the outcome of the meet or has the old attitude that "the score does not count, only the way you play the game," will seldom produce teams that do their best under pressure. Her girls will probably never know what it means to go all out or put forth the maximum effort at crucial times. Of course a team wants to win. This is a natural goal and should be encouraged at every competition.

In gymnastics, winning often depends upon insuring that every performer is physically relaxed but emotionally "up" for her turn on the apparatus. To produce this delicate balance is one of the most difficult jobs a coach has. Coaches who have natural talent in this area can produce great teams even if the skill level is not oustandingly high. Understanding every girl's personal motives for being on the team and applying psychological tools in order to produce in her the desired state of mind before a competition has been called one of the greatest arts in coaching.

Girls join gymnastics teams for various reasons. Since simple dedication to a sport is not yet completely acceptable in a girl in our society, a team is usually composed of individuals who are there for distinctly different reasons. The personality types and apparent motivations of these girls can be so varied that it may take a coach some time to see through all the facades and get to the real motivations of the girls on her team. Most girls will turn out to be fairly uncomplicated and easy to work with. Despite their individual reasons for joining the team, these athletes generally enjoy the sport and wish to make it a part of their lives for a certain number of years. However, they tend to be more individualistic and independent than girls participating in traditional team sports.

The atypical athlete is not quite as easy to understand or handle. She can end up either greatly contributing to or greatly disrupting the work of a team. Understanding the atypical athletic and her motivations is essential to the coach if she wants to provide successful athletic experiences to all her team members.

Very few in-depth studies have been made of the personalities or motivations of girl athletes who engage seriously in one selected sport.

Talking in general terms and using extremes to illustrate the point, here are some of the motivational categories of atypical girl athletes:

1. The "Queen Bee." This girl is usually a cheerleader, president of this, chairman of the other, and the beauty queen of something else. Very often she is one of the most popular and active girls in school. She decides to give gymnastics a try because she has tried almost everything else and is looking for new outlets for her energies. The Queen Bee has many friends and many interests in life, so that she seldom allows enough time to concentrate seriously on any one thing. This gymnast has a hard time following training regulations or coming to the required number of practices. Since she is self-reliant and a leader in her own right, she usually does not need the moral support of a coach and can be put into a proper frame of mind for competition by teammates or an eagerly responsive audience. Usually talented and a great "ham," the Queen Bee always seems to get by, but cannot be depended upon to deliver an all-out performance when the team needs it.

Girls like this can be very trying to a dedicated coach, since they always seem to come up with excuses for not working as hard as the coach desires. Yet they are likable personalities and may have great potential. Teams just beginning in gymnastics may be in a great need of this type of girl, but in serious competitive situations she can become a demoralizing influence. A coach may have to take a firm stand with a team member of this type, even if it results in losing her in the long run.

2. The Athlete Who Resists Coaching. This type of athlete has usually been a "child prodigy," has had previous private coaching, or comes from a small town, where she was the best, into a big school or club, where she may have to fight for her position. Sometimes she has been exploited by a previous coach and so has lost confidence in adult guidance and in coaches in general. Other times she is certain that nobody can take the place of her previous coach and tends to view all other coaches with suspicion.

Whatever the reason, the girl is suspicious of the new situation and may even openly resist any help by the new coach. This type of team member is usually a loner and depends mostly on herself. She does not develop fast friendships among the team. At the beginning, the other members of the team may even resent her for not having enough team spirit or not becoming a member of the established group.

Trying to get through to a girl who resists coaching requires self-discipline and patience on the part of the coach, especially if the performer happens to be quite advanced in her skills and could contribute greatly to a unified team effort. Oglivie and Tutko[3] recommend the following approach:

   a. Remain at a physical distance; don't force yourself upon her.
   b. Respond to her slightest approaches with warmth and acceptance.
   c. Reduce spoken communication to a minimum and answer in single words if possible.
   d. Make a favorable comment every now and then (but only if it is honestly deserved), preferably in an off-hand fashion. Here too, keep the words at minimum.
   e. Wait. If everything has been successful, she will come to you eventually and could turn out to be one of the best members of the team.

3. The Success-Oriented, Self-Centered Athlete. This girl can be either a great help or a great nuisance on the team. Every gymnast should be to some extent success-oriented and, because of the individual nature

3. *Op. cit.,* p. 44.

of the sport, will be somewhat self-centered, especially when compared to team-sport-oriented girls. If a coach succeeds in channeling these attributes in a constructive way, the girl could be a great gymnast. Unchecked, the same personality traits can easily turn her into an extremely unlikable and uncooperative person.

The success-oriented athlete should be kept challenged by the sport, but should not be pushed beyond her capacity before she is ready for it. Success is very important to this girl. In gymnastics, success is traditionally measured by judges' scores earned in competition. If the routine of this gymnast is too difficult for her to handle and she scores constantly too low because of major breaks or falls, her self-esteem is lessened and she is likely to strike back at the coach with moods or temper tantrums. On the other hand, if she finds success and is constantly challenged by a well-planned program of progressions, she can be the hardest worker in the gym, willing to practice seven days a week and dedicate herself totally to the sport.

This gymnast is not usually a patient teacher of lesser skilled teammates but works well with girls at her own skill level. If the rest of the group is below her level, the coach should try to spend some extra time with her outside of regular practice hours. This time will usually turn out to be very well spent.

Another important thing to a success-oriented girl is the development of a personal goal in the sport. The coach should be honest with her in evaluating her chances for advanced work and explain the sacrifices involved in the process. The gymnast should be encouraged to aim for higher and higher personal scores, which will, incidentally, also benefit the team. Putting the team score first will not usually motivate this athlete sufficiently. She needs a goal more directly related to her as a person.

Coaches who are very strongly oriented toward the team spirit concept will have a more difficult time liking and understanding a success-oriented, self-centered athlete. Yet the presence of this hard-working and single-minded girl can do wonders for the entire team if the coach sets up a proper atmosphere and keeps internal jealousies from developing.

It is not easy for a coach to have an *exceptionally gifted* success-oriented athlete on her team and do justice to her talents without sacrificing the rest of the team. Very often the girl needs special handling and can stretch a coach's patience to the limit. However, this is the material from which star gymnasts are made and developed. Can a coach waste such a talent? Is it her duty to give more of herself to this girl or should she recognize her own limitations of time and skill and send the student on to someone who specializes in advanced individual instruction? The answers to these questions often reveal the personality and motivations of the coach herself and her relationship to the sport.

4. The "Psyched-Out" Athlete. The hyper-anxious athlete who seems to burn herself out psychologically prior to actual competition is actually her own worst enemy. This girl becomes very tense prior to a meet. Her movements lack their usual free-flowing quality and become jerky. A set position of jaw muscles can be another external sign. The highly anxious athlete loses her power of concentration and begins to respond to a whole range of distracting stimuli. She also becomes overly sensitive to any good-natured kidding by her teammates, especially if the possibility of failure is mentioned. Oglivie and Tutko recommend six actions. In brief, they are as follows: (1) Be cautious in your use of criticism with this athlete. (2) Watch your personal moods and feelings. This athlete can be very sensitive to the moods of others, often looking for signs of rejection. (3) Gather your composure before approaching her, since any anxiety from your part will add to hers. (4) Give a chance to this girl to talk and vent her feelings before her turn comes to compete. Be a good listener. (5) Underplay her

role in the relation to the team's success. The "psyched out" athlete usually has an exaggerated need to take on responsibility and guilt for the team failure. If possible, she should not be given the additional burden of the team leadership. Being the captain may add to her anxiety and assumed responsibility for the performance of the entire team. (6) Share as much of her emotional load as possible without being untruthful or overly protective.

This is only a short and admittedly incomplete list of personality traits and motivations of atypical girl athletes. Stereotypes are, of course, exceptional; most girls fall somewhere between the types discussed.

It is important to the coach to understand the aims and motivations of all the girls on her team if she hopes to mold them into a closely working unit. In practice situations, the coach has to know how far to push and how severely to criticize each girl on the team. Most girls will benefit from being pushed, but some personality types may react negatively toward it. A success-oriented girl, for example, wants to be pushed and will usually do her best under some type of pressure. Last-minute instructions from the coach can put her into a proper frame of mind for competition, and she usually wants an immediate evaluation of her performance afterwards.

A "psyched-out" athlete needs to be relaxed before her turn comes. The coach can try to talk to her about completely unrelated things and minimize the importance of the competition. Immediately afterwards, she needs encouragement, not a complete analysis of her weak and strong points during the presentation.

The "queen bee," on the other hand, may not need anything from the coach before or after the competition. She gets her important reactions from the audience and can dismiss a low score as "just one of those things."

An athlete who resists coaching should be left alone

immediately prior to her performance. The coach should be physically present if necessary but should say as little as possible. If the girl prefers to have a competent teammate spot her, the coach should not display hurt feelings or displeasure. Criticisms after the completion of the routine should be carefully and constructively worded and given in an unexcited manner.

In large meets the order of competition is usually drawn at random and the coach has no influence over it. However, in dual or three-way meet situations a coach is usually asked to submit her line-up ahead of time, indicating the competitive order of her girls. Deciding upon this order is another phase of the coach's work in which knowledge of the personalities of the girls and their reactions under stress will help her to make the best decision.

Though the general trend is to place the weakest girl first and the strongest one last, there are cases in which this will not work out to the best advantage of the team. The first competitor usually sets the tone for that event, as far as her team is concerned. She should be able to give a steady and relaxed performance. Allowing an unsteady or overly nervous girl to go first, could upset the entire team.

The last performer should also be a steady one: a girl with something extra to give, either in her skills or in the way of presenting them. There are few things more deflating to the morale of the team than finishing an event with a poor, nervous performer. If the competition is close, the last girl should be one who can come through under pressure.

The "queen bee" often makes a good first girl. In the proper mood, she can really warm up the audience and judges. However, she is not the best risk for the last position if the competition is close.

The competitor who resists coaching might do equally well in either position, providing she is where she really belongs as far as her skills are concerned. She may not react well to position changes for the sake of team strategy if it removes her from her true position in the line-up.

A success-oriented girl often performs better under pressure, *if* she is well prepared and secure in her routine. Under these circumstances, she seems to enjoy tight spots and close competition. If the competition is not close, the coach can have her try out a new move in her routine, providing the needed challenge in this manner.

The "psyched-out" athlete should go neither first or last, but be tucked somewhere in the middle. If possible, she should be given a chance to follow a weaker performer either on her own team or, even better, among the opposing girls. The worst position for her is that following a highly skilled or otherwise spectacular gymnast.

Coaching a team is an extremely challenging and ever-changing job. What works today may not work tomorrow. The number of new and different situations that can arise is impossible to calculate, in view of the complexities of the human nature and the differing personalities of the girls involved. A coach who is secure within herself and sensitive to the needs of her students will never find this job dull or routine, even after many years of coaching the same sport. Every year brings different situations and a wide variety of new personalities to be dealt with, molded, and developed to the best of her ability. The sensitive coach will become an amateur psychologist, whether she knows it or not, and will definitely have some influence over her team members in their most impressionable years. In order to take on this great responsibility, a coach should first be at peace with herself, so that she can concentrate on the reactions of her students.

Patsy Neal has a direct and forthright way of summing it all up:

The coach's foremost responsibility is to her team. To fulfill this responsibility, she must be adaptable, imaginative, creative and capable of being a dynamic leader as well as a friend and a slave driver.

If the coach can integrate her needs with those of her players and come out with an easy relationship both with herself and with those she is coaching, then she can consider her job as being well done.

She will find that coaching can be the most satisfying and challenging work there is.[4]

4. *Op. cit,* pp. 9-10.

11

Training and Certification of Judges

JACQUELYN UPHUES FIE

The Women's Gymnastic Certification Committee (DGWS-USGF), with full approval and recognition by the USA National Gymnastics Commission, is now conducting a nation-wide program for the certification of gymnastics judges. Since the spring of 1969 both the USGF and the DGWS have administered these tests throughout the nation. Each organization is responsible for publicizing its own certification dates.

Depending on the sponsoring organization, notice of the tests may be given on a local, state, district, or regional basis. For information on the dates and locations' of upcoming tests, one may contact the following officials:

1. Local Officiating Services Area Board (OSA)
2. State DGWS Gymnastics Chairman
3. State USGF Chairman
4. Regional USGF Chairman
5. Chairman of the Women's Gymnastic Certification Committee (DGWS-USGF)
6. Regional Gymnastic Newsletter Services

In addition, training programs for judges preparing to take the certification examination are offered separately by the DGWS and the USGF. For schedules and guidelines for judges' training workshops, the following offices should be contacted:

DGWS: OSA Local Board
        (For address check current DGWS
        Gymnastics Guide)

USGF: Judges' Training Committee,
        Chairman
        (Mrs. Delene Darst)
        c/o The United States
        Gymnastic Federation
        P.O. Box 4699
        Tucson, Arizona 85717

The clinics and workshops for the training of judges sponsored by these two organizations give instruction and review all pertinent information. Study materials used are National USGF/DGWS Compulsory Routines for Girls, 1972-76, the FIG Code of Points and Supplemental Study Guide plus the 1971 Complement, and the 1972 Judging Guide for Women.

A study of the exactness of the prescribed exercises—the National USGF/DGWS Compulsory Routines for Girls—is followed by a detailed study of the Table of Penalties and Deductions. Actual practice in judging compulsories is included in the training program.

The National Compulsory Routines are available from:

DGWS: DGWS Current Gymnastic Guide
      American Association for Health,
        Physical Education and Recreation
      1201 Sixteenth Street, N.W.
      Washington, D.C. 20036

USGF: USGF Age Group Competition,
Chairman
Miss Betty Meyer
c/o USGF
P.O. Box 4699
Tucson, Arizona 85717

The official FIG Code of Points plus 1971 Complement and the 1972 Judging Guide for Women are available from:

USGF Office
P.O. Box 4699
Tucson, Arizona 85717

A thorough knowledge of the entire Code of Points and the ability to apply this memorized information rapidly and fairly are of the utmost importance. All perspective judges should participate in as many workshops and clinics as possible and take advantage of every opportunity to judge performances during practice sessions and actual competitions. Views should be discussed continually with coaches, gymnasts, and other judges. Meets and workshops should be attended regularly to keep abreast of new trends, difficulties, combinations, and styles. Judging should be practiced at all levels: beginning, intermediate, and advanced. Actual judging experience, supervised by a nationally or internationally rated official or clinic instructor, is the most beneficial preparation for the certification examination.

Following are some pertinent rules and policies of the Women's Gymnastic Certification Committee:

Examination Cost: $3.00 per examinee
Ratings: Local, Regional, and National (These ratings refer to the skill of the judge and not to a geographical area.)
  1. Local: qualified to judge any competition in any geographical area with the exception of Elite (international division). Minimum age requirement: 18 years. Men are eligible for local ratings only.
  2. Regional: qualified to judge any competition, compulsory and optional, in any geographical area with the exception of Elite. Minimum age requirement: 18 years.
  3. National: qualified to judge any competition in any geographical area. Minimum age requirement: 20 years.

Length of Certification and Requirements (a certification year extends from September 1 to August 30):
  1. Certification length is based on Olympic years: anyone who qualifies between the present time and the next Olympiad will be certified until December of that Olympic year.
  2. All certified judges must requalify by taking the total examination at the end of their certification period.
  3. Certified officials are required to judge three meets per year or a total of six within a two-year period to maintain status.

Any examinee who scores lower than 70% on the theoretical or 50% on the practical examination is not eligible to be certified. The following minimum scores must be met on both parts of the examination in order to earn the appropriate rating:

National: 90% T — 80% P
Regional: 80% T — 65% P
Local: 70% T — 50% P

The examinee may retest only once during a certification year and no sooner than four weeks after the initial testing. She may retest on either the practical, theoretical, or both areas of the examination.

A current list of certified judges is available through the Certification Coordinator of the Women's Gymnastics Certification Commitee of the USGF-DGWS.

This system of certification and the requirement that active status be maintained will establish and sus- tain a high professional level for judges. At the same time the total program of compulsory and optional gymnastics from local to elite levels will accelerate in quantity and quality as a result of the trained pro- fessional guidance rendered by certified judges.

DATE DUE